The Washington Lawyer

The Washington Lawyer

A series of lectures delivered under the auspices of the Julius Rosenthal Foundation at Northwestern University School of Law, in April 1952

by

CHARLES A. HORSKY

OF THE DISTRICT OF COLUMBIA BAR

GREENWOOD PRESS, PUBLISHERS
WESTPORT, CONNECTICUT

Library of Congress Cataloging in Publication Data

Horsky, Charles Antone.
The Washington lawyer.

Reprint of the ed. published by Little, Brown, Boston.
Includes bibliographical references.
1. Lawyers--District of Columbia--Addresses, essays, lectures. 2. Lobbying--United States--Addresses, essays, lectures. 3. United States--Executive departments--Addresses, essays, lectures. 4. Administrative courts--United States--Addresses, essays, lectures. I. Title.
KF300.H65 1981 349.73'023'753 81-646
ISBN 0-313-22736-5 (lib. bdg.) AACR1

Reprinted with the permission of Northwestern University School of Law.

Reprinted in 1981 by Greenwood Press
A division of Congressional Information Service, Inc.
88 Post Road West, Westport, Connecticut 06881

Printed in the United States of America

10 9 8 7 6 5 4 3 2

Foreword

The Julius Rosenthal Foundation for General Law

JULIUS ROSENTHAL, an eminent and beloved member of the Chicago bar, was born in Germany on September 17, 1828. He pursued his studies at the Universities of Heidelberg and Freiburg, came to Chicago in July, 1854, and was admitted to the bar in 1860. He was especially prominent as a practitioner in the law of wills and in probate and real estate law. As librarian of the Chicago Law Institute from 1867 to 1877 and again from 1888 to 1903, and as its president from 1878 to 1880, he was chiefly responsible for its development. He was a member of the First Board of State Law Examiners of Illinois, and its secretary from 1897 to 1899. He died May 14, 1905.

Julius Rosenthal was a lawyer of great learning

and rare scholarly attainments. He labored long and earnestly to establish the highest standards of legal scholarship. Throughout his career, his interest in the Northwestern University School of Law was constantly manifested.

To honor his memory the Julius Rosenthal Foundation for General Law was established in 1919 by his son, Lessing Rosenthal, his daughter, Mrs. George Pick, and Charles H. Hamill, Max Hart, Harry Hart, Mark Cresap, Frank M. Peters, Leo P. Wormser, F. Howard Eldridge, Willard L. King, Magnus Myres, Mrs. Joseph Schaffner, and Mrs. Otto L. Schmidt, all of Chicago, and the Honorable Julian W. Mack, of New York. Additional funds were provided under the will of Lessing Rosenthal, who died in 1949. The income derived from the Foundation is, among other uses, applicable to the cultivation of legal literature, and particularly to the publication of meritorious essays, monographs, and books of a scientific or practical nature concerning the law; to the aid or encouragement of research in the field of legal literature and the preparation for publication of the results of such research; and to the delivery and publication of lectures on subjects concerning the law.

Preface

A DECADE or more of discussions with law students considering a career as a Washington lawyer has required some answer to the questions, What do Washington lawyers do, and how do they do it? The invitation to deliver these lectures furnished the occasion for an organization of these random introspective analyses, and, once the invitation was accepted, furnished the necessary impetus as well.

There is much of Washington law practice, of course, with which the lectures do not deal at all. There is much more where the author's individual experience has no doubt colored both the description and the analysis. Complete objectivity, and anything like adequate information, present singular difficulties in writing of the practice of law. I venture to think that the difficulties are compounded in treating the Washington lawyer.

My thanks are due to the several Washington lawyers who read and criticized portions of the lectures, and particularly to the researches and many helpful suggestions of Albert M. Sacks and Louis Cox. And one would be thankless indeed to fail to mention the memorable hospitality of the Northwestern Law School faculty, particularly Dean Harold C. Havighurst and the faculty committee on the lectures, Professors Brunson MacChesney, W. Willard Wirtz and Nathaniel L. Nathanson.

C.A.H.

Washington, D.C.
September, 1952

Contents

The Washington Lawyer

I. General Characteristics of Washington Practice; Judicial and Legislative Activities

IN AN EARLIER TIME it was common, when publishing a book, to buttress the title with a sometimes lengthy subtitle. If I were to do this, I would call this book "The Washington Lawyer, or, Some Aspects of the Problems Confronting That Part of the Legal Profession Which Is Particularly Affected by the Operation of the Federal Government." In discussing the Washington lawyer, we are dealing with a sort of by-product of those forces that have perhaps produced a new kind of political administration in this country; the character of his work is largely shaped by the nature of modern federal government itself. What I hope to do, then, is to sketch the effect on this one small segment of society of the growth and extension of our federal government.

Perhaps a more realistic subtitle would be "Where Angels Fear to Tread." There are hazards in any description of what lawyers do, or should do. Lawyers, as we know perhaps too well, have authored and have as their peculiar province, an enormous amount of writings – books, articles, periodicals, and decisions – in which they are always prolific and often prolix. Yet seldom does a lawyer venture to write about what lawyers do. There are two obstacles.

First, the lawyer is never privileged to reveal matters which he has learned from his client as a lawyer. Even as to the matters which are not strictly within the scope of the attorney-client privilege – and it is the client's privilege – the lawyer is pretty well inhibited from the sort of account that might be made, for example, of the military operation that resulted in the capture of Iwo Jima. The grand strategy, the tactical maneuvers, the efforts to conceal weak points, the questions which were not asked of the witnesses and the arguments which were not made to the court, are all largely foreclosed from exposition and analysis. Time relaxes those bonds very slowly.

Second, in trying to describe a broad picture,

there is the very considerable danger of winding up by saying nothing at all. Most of "what lawyers do" is too well-known to be worth restatement. What remains is so *ad hoc*, so tailored to the needs of the particular problem confronting the particular client, that any generalization may be as misleading as it is enlightening. We shall see whether there is any path between the Scylla of tedious platitude and the Charybdis of professional inhibitions.

When we talk only of the Washington lawyer the task is somewhat easier, because we are dealing with only a portion of the bar, and one whose functions, even in the generalizing, reveal many facets of interest because they reflect the day-by-day working out of government. That, however, is counterbalanced by the wide diversity of activities of even this group, and the consequent difficulty of fairly describing what other Washington lawyers do in their own sphere. The Washington lawyer would no doubt be different through other eyes than mine. But let us be certain, at the outset, that we define our class. What is a "Washington lawyer"?

I do not propose to use the term simply to mean a lawyer in Washington. There is a large group of lawyers in Washington — the lawyers who work for the United States and District of Columbia Governments — with which I am not concerned, at least not for present purposes. Although they are in a sense the mirror in which is reflected almost everything which I will have to say about their brethren in private practice, let us put them to one side.

Nor am I concerned with the lawyers who practice in Washington because Washington, as a community of about 800,000 people, requires private legal services as does any other community. People in Washington make contracts, commit crimes and torts, die testate or intestate, and do or fail to do all of the variety of things which are the concern of lawyers everywhere.

There remain those lawyers who practice in Washington because it is the seat of the federal government. Their work is characterized by the direct impact of that government on their clients. These are the Washington lawyers, as we shall consider them.

I hasten to admit that this is an arbitrary classification, and that it is neither static nor clear-cut. One of these Washington lawyers may hurry back to his office from a hearing at the Federal Power Commission to draw a will, or to foreclose a mortgage. Most Washington law firms, and certainly all the larger ones, have a local as well as a national clientele. But though it may be impossible to state categorically whether a given attorney is a Washington lawyer, and though the limits of the group are so blurred and shifting as to frustrate sharp definition, Washington lawyers as I mean to write of them do exist, and in large, if uncertain, numbers.

Statistics are, of course, apt to prove treacherous, but the most reliable figures available [1] serve to indicate something of the size of this group. Here are a few round figures.

There are about 170,000 lawyers in the United States, or roughly one lawyer to every 883 persons. Exclusive of those holding public office, there are slightly over 3700 lawyers in Washington; on the basis of 1949 figures this means there is one lawyer in the District for every 183 persons. In contrast, the corresponding ratio in New York City is about one to 415. To put these figures in a more meaningful way, if we assume that the tendency of the bar to concentrate in large cities makes for an approximate ratio of one to 500, there are nearly three times as many nongovernment lawyers in Washington as one would expect to find in a city of equivalent size. Clearly Washington must have a very considerable group of lawyers whose practice is not devoted to the affairs of the community in which it is located.

There is another factor which thwarts precise delineation of this part of the profession. Just as all lawyers in Washington are not Washington lawyers, so there are many who meet our definition of Washington lawyers but who do not work in Washington, D.C. We are dealing with those whose legal practice is largely caused by the direct impact of the federal government on the interests of their clients. Hence, Washington lawyers, like the government itself, may be found in Dallas or Seattle, in Detroit or Savannah. More particularly, they will be found in large firms throughout the country which are more or less comparable to the large law offices in New York and Chicago. The experience of the Cravath firm in New York is certainly not atypical:

> By far the greatest single part of the practice of the firm since 1928 has had to do with the efforts of clients to comply with Federal legislation and to accommodate their businesses to the vagaries of the many Federal regulatory agencies and executive departments.[2]

The firm in New Orleans which specializes in tax practice, the firm in San Francisco which finds the operations of the Maritime Administration at the root of its client's difficulties, and the firm in Boston advising a client enmeshed in the toils of Securities and Exchange Commission regulations all contain Washington lawyers.

But to keep the consideration of our general topic – the congeries of lawyers' problems raised by the broadening impact of the federal government on national life – within manageable scope, it is necessary simply to acknowledge that the topic is too broad to treat within the range of this small volume, and to focus particularly, though not exclusively, on the Washington lawyer who has his office in Washington. That will be more than enough.

The reader may wonder whether there is any point to this classification – whether the Washington lawyer, as I have defined him, is significantly different from the remainder of the bar. That question, of course, is precisely what I shall explore.

Nevertheless, even at the start, this can be said: The Washington lawyer represents a recent development in the legal profession sufficiently distinctive to repay separate consideration, because he has become an essential part of our present scheme of government. His function, broadly, is that of principal interpreter between government and private person, explaining to each the needs, desires and demands of the other. His corollary function is that of seeking to adjust the conflicts that inevitably arise.

These roles may seem too ambitiously stated, and I am aware that there is always a danger of overstating the significance of a group of which one is a member. I am aware, too, that these functions have not been assumed by the Washington lawyer deliberately, perhaps not even consciously. He acts, for the most part, only when some client wants help on a problem which in some way relates to government. Yet, in the course of acting on behalf of his *client*, the lawyer has an important influence on *government*. We have recognized that the advocate in the courtroom is an essential aid to the court's function. The Washington lawyer extends this assistance to the legislative, executive and administrative processes. As in the past the lawyer has aided the court, so today the Washington lawyer aids the government, in its other branches.

We shall test this thesis as we proceed, against the descriptive detail of what Washington lawyers do. To the extent that it proves valid, it may help to give meaning to what otherwise would seem merely anecdotal. The important implication of the thesis, however, lies deeper. If Washington lawyers have the kind of role I have described, it is important that they realize and analyze it, the better to fulfill it. Even the abuses of that role – the various practices which today come under the broad label of "influence-peddling" – can best be examined after the Washington lawyer's proper function is understood. I do not promise the ultimate analysis. But we can ask some critical questions, and perhaps venture a few evaluations and conclusions.

Before we come to these larger questions – indeed before we can even formulate them with any precision – we need to answer the question, What does the Washington lawyer do? But we can get some help, at least in a preliminary way, by briefly considering historical background. Why has the Washington bar developed as it has?

Lawyers, perhaps more than members of any other profession, reflect the character of the society in which they operate. Let me illustrate by contrasting the nature of the profession in Italy, as described by a recent writer:

> Italy has witnessed during the last few years the well-known phenomenon of the concentration of the better and larger part of the legal practice in the hands of a few lawyers; yet, most Italian practitioners, even the busiest, practice alone or with one or two assistants. Without being disrespectful or critical, it may be said that Italian lawyers are still organized like artisans rather than like entrepreneurs. This is still possible because the economic, business, and financial structure of the country is much less complicated and diversified than that of the United States.[3]

I said at the beginning that the Washington lawyer is a sort of by-product of those forces which have produced a new kind of government in this country. Perhaps I might better have said that insofar as he represents a distinct segment of the American bar, he affords a peculiarly vivid illustration of change in the nature of the economy effecting changes in the practice of a profession noted for its adherence to tradition. However this may be, the development of the Washington bar and the nature of its work have as root causes the economic forces which have shaped so much of recent American history.

It would serve no present purpose to do more than suggest the nature of these forces. They are familiar, at least in a general way, to us all: they are subsumed under such captions as "industrial revolution," "economic integration," and the like. The salient feature of the modern American economy is an interdependence of component parts which is scarcely susceptible of exaggeration. During the past fifty years, the mass production techniques of industry have impinged on almost every field of economic endeavor; specialization and integration now are characteristics of nearly every sphere of human activity.

The process of simultaneous fractionalization of functions and unification of interests, most marked in industry, has extended into the service field as well. Banking and retail marketing, for example, have felt the influence of combination and diversification; and where common ownership or control remains absent, integration advances through trade associations, pooling arrangements, and the like. Even in agriculture, an area where individual producing units are notably resistant to collective self-regulation, area crop specialization and farm and marketing cooperatives bear witness to the same tendencies.

The result of all this is the creation of an increasingly intricate complex of finely meshed economic balances. Any official of a government agency such as the Office of Price Stabilization, which has attempted to modify the nice adjustments of this complex, can testify that the economy as a whole displays an organic sensitiveness to the slightest dislocation of any one of its parts. Stated in simplest terms, what a man does today – far more than ever before – makes a difference in the lives of other men.

The lawyer's work is a function of this pattern of economic development. The business of the lawyer is human conflicts, actual or threatened. The nature of his practice stems from the nature of those conflicts. In earlier days, the typical conflict involved but one clear-cut, definite interest opposed to another clear-cut interest, and the lawyer's task was largely that of an advocate, championing his side. Today, far more frequently, situations of clear-cut conflict become rare and a multiplicity of overlapping interests confronts the attorney. The skills of the advocate must be supplemented by the skills of the negotiator; forensic talent yields to executive talent. The lawyer's task becomes more and more one of reducing the friction in a complex of competing interests.

Before we examine the consequences of this development on the Washington bar in particular, let us also take note of the revolution in government that has paralleled the revolution in industry and commerce. A quotation will at once describe the situation, and serve to warn against overstatement:

> The Government, having become more active in the last twenty years, and having embarked in every species of undertaking which it had never thought of before, was at last become the greatest contractor of public works in the country; the number of persons who had pecuniary transactions with the state, who were interested in governmental loans, live by government wages, or speculate in government contracts, had prodigiously increased. Never before had the fortune of the nation and the fortunes of private persons been so much intermingled.

The need for caution will be apparent when I tell you that the author is Alexis de Tocqueville,[4] and the description is of the French government in the late eighteenth century. Intensive and extensive government on a national scale has not been a peculiarly American phenomenon. Indeed, it developed in the United States much later than in countries whose economic and political growth followed the customary pattern of feudalism crystallizing into strong and pervasive centralized government. Nonetheless, its emergence here in the first half of the twentieth century, slowly at first and with accelerated speed in the 1930's and 1940's, is one of the most momentous facts of our time.

It has truly been a governmental revolution. A half-century ago statutes were considered at the Harvard Law School as "excrescences on the pure body of the common law." Today they and the corps of commissions, bureaus and boards created to interpret and administer their provisions have crowded the buildings of Washington and exhausted anyone who has sought to master their alphabetical profusion. They are the clearest indicia of a government which governs so much more than it did that it can fairly be called something new in America.

In Washington, these effects have been so accentuated that they have brought into being a bar which is, in many respects, unique. No one doubts, of course, that this group has grown since 1933, when the New Deal agencies began to multiply. It expanded rapidly with the emergency agencies of World War II. I venture to suggest, however, that many persons may not appreciate the extent to which the Washington lawyer did *not* exist before 1933, despite the temporary effects of World War I.

In no area have I felt more keenly the absence of historical material on the work of lawyers than in trying to document that statement. That it is true is vouchsafed by my older brethren, but I have found no way in which to obtain any independent or contemporary evaluation of the Washington bar of thirty or thirty-five years ago.

Indeed, it is far easier to describe the bar as it existed in the District of Columbia in 1820 than as it existed in 1920. There has been enough curiosity about the beginnings of things to have stimulated inquiry into the very early days — the first cases, the first judges, the first persons to be admitted to practice. They were complex days, too, with four sets of laws being administered by the Washington courts — the Maryland law for that part of the District ceded by Maryland, the Virginia law for that part ceded by Virginia, the English common law to fill the gaps in both, and overriding all of them the statutory law passed by or for the District of Columbia itself. A recounting of the events and personalities of the very early days would make pleasant reading.

What is lacking, however, is any intermediate description adequate to isolate the Washington lawyer, as we use the term, from his local brethren. We can only indicate the outside possibilities of the effect of the presence of the federal government. Some federal agencies have existed practically from the beginning, and have attracted their own more or less distinctive bars. Even the earliest publications, shortly after the Civil War, of that estimable team, Martindale and Hubbell, contain notices of Washington patent attorneys. In 1880, of the four Washington firms which published legal notices in Hubbell, two specialized in patent law, the other two in collections. Five years later patent firms were four out of seven, and the concentration of patent law firms continued for many years. Indeed, many of the early giants of that bar practiced in Washington until ease of transportation and communication made it possible for them to be in New York, Boston, Chicago, and elsewhere.

Again there appears to have been a considerable group who practiced before the General Land Office. Public land matters are still a fertile field for Washington lawyers, particularly in connection with subsurface oil and mineral rights, but probably the work is incomparably less significant than it was in the early days when the disposition of the vast public domain posed one of the great perennial political issues of the time. A legal notice in Hubbell in 1895 still carried the echoes of the Civil War: "Pensions secured for soldiers, sailors, widows, parents and minor children. Write for particulars." Many lawyers professed special experience in representing clients before committees of the House and Senate. From Civil War days on, the Court of Claims, then unique in jurisdiction and largely different in procedure, seems to have had a bar of its own.[5] But despite this miscellany of indications that there were groups of lawyers in Washington whose work was marked by its close relation to governmental activities, there is too little evidence to substantiate even a guess as to whether there was anything which we might fairly call a bar of Washington lawyers.

By 1915, however, the beginnings of such a bar are evident. Of the 65 firms listed in Hubbell, 9 are in the familiar patent field, but one firm announces its special competence in practice before the Interstate Commerce Commission, and another in practice under the Pure Food and Drug Act. In the same year, Martindale carried the announcement of another firm which gave special attention to "Income tax and other Internal Revenue Matters." I have heard the story, however, of the attorney who in 1917 declined a better legal position in the Bureau of Internal Revenue than he then held in the War Department, because he was convinced it could only be temporary; the income tax would certainly be repealed shortly after the war.

Tax practice, nonetheless, soon became a leading part of the work of the Washington lawyer during the 1920's. This, of course, is what might be expected, because from World War I until 1933, income and excess profits taxes tended to become the principal manifestation of the interventionist tendencies of modern government. There were other government cases but they were largely concerned with traditional operations of government — tariff matters, copyright cases, antitrust matters, visas, naturalization and immigration proceedings, and advice or appearances in connection with legislation. Relatively speaking, however, they were not numerous. Although the beginnings of the modern Washington lawyer can be discerned as far back as thirty years ago, I think it fair to say that only in the last two decades has he become numerous and important enough to warrant treatment as a distinctive element of the American bar.[6]

But it is high time, no doubt, that we come to grips with the substantive question — What do Washington lawyers do, today? History is interesting, and I only wish there were more of it, but what most concerns us now is the present. Washington lawyers are handling, today, the present problems of their present clients. What kinds of activities does that involve?

As I mentioned at the outset, it is difficult to generalize. The functions of the Washington lawyer do not lend themselves to scientific classification, nor are there many Q.E.D.'s. To afford some sort of pattern it has seemed to me feasible to tie the discussion to the conventional divisions of government.

On the judicial side – the traditional bailiwick of the lawyer – we can examine the relationship of the Washington lawyer to the courts, in Washington in particular, but also to those located elsewhere. On the legislative side, we shall discuss lobbying, not in its asserted venal sense, but in its broad aspects. On the executive side, we shall analyze the function of the lawyer both before the various executive departments and their divisions and before those agencies which exercise a blend of legislative, executive and judicial power.

Let us consider, then, the relation of the Washington lawyer to the courts. Courts are, after all, what one thinks of when one thinks of lawyers. And it is perhaps significant, in understanding the Washington lawyer, that we will be able to conclude that this is the area of his activities in which he is least unusual.

Indeed, we might almost generalize by stating that the Washington lawyer has no special relationship to the Washington courts, and let it go at that. The very absence of special relationship, however, in the areas where it exists, is worthy of at least brief comment, and there are a few respects in which our generalization is not true.

Moreover, here we have had a definite change from the past. The early days of the Supreme Court, for example, were the days of a true Supreme Court bar. I have made no attempt at tabulations, but without doubt, in the important cases during the Court's first fifty years one could reasonably expect to find among counsel names such as Pinkney, Wirt, Webster, Hopkinson, Dexter, Sergeant, Ogden and Wheaton.[7] Arguments then were not the mere one hour per side to which we are now accustomed; often a case would consume several days, and several counsel would participate on each side. Briefs, of course, were not printed, nor were the records. Clients might understandably believe that when oral presentation had such significance, those of the golden tongue as well as of the legal mind were to be retained whenever they could be afforded. Charles Warren has pointed out that in the early nineteenth century,

> The difficulties attendant on travelling to Washington in those ante-railroad days were reflected by the immense number of cases argued by eminent counsel residing in the District of Columbia. Probably from one-fifth to one-fourth of all the cases appearing in the volumes of the reporters, Henry Wheaton and Richard Peters, during this period, were argued by Francis

Scott Key, John Law, Thomas Swann, Walter Jones or Richard S. Coxe – all local counsel residing in or about Washington.[8]

Indeed, there were at least half-serious complaints that the Washington bar exerted an undue influence on the Court. During a debate on a bill introduced in 1819 to relieve the Supreme Court Justices of circuit duty, Senator Lacock of Pennsylvania foresaw that if the Justices, being elderly men, were not required occasionally to leave Washington, they would become the mere tools of the Washington lawyer:

". . . These weaknesses incident to old age will be discovered and practised upon by the lawyer willing to make the most of his profession, and located in the same city, holding daily and familiar intercourse with the Judges. And thus, your Court may become subservient to the Washington Bar. The Judges, bound down by the weight of years, will be willing to find a staff to lean upon; and the opinion of the Washington Bar is made the law of the land. A knot of attorneys at or near the seat of Government having gained the ear, and secured the confidence of the Court, will banish all competition from abroad."[9]

Senator Lacock can rest in peace; his fears were groundless. If there has been any Supreme Court bar for the past fifty years, it has been confined to the attorneys in the Department of Justice, particularly those in the office of the Solicitor General. There are, of course, lawyers who argue in that Court more frequently than others do, but those outside the government who have averaged two arguments per term over a span of ten years could probably be counted on the fingers of one hand. Ease of travel and the simple numerical increase in the number of lawyers who must divide among them the limited number of cases which a single Court can hear and determine take care of that.

The other peculiarly Washington judicial tribunal — the Court of Claims — has retained, to a much greater degree, the bar which quickly developed after its creation. Until the recent revision of its rules, it had a mode of procedure radically different from other federal courts, and even now a lawyer who is handling his tenth case before it is no doubt far more comfortable than one who is handling his first. Moreover, the Court of Claims sits only in Washington, and it is probably true that when a person wants to sue in that court, or when an attorney elsewhere in the United States has a client who wants to sue there, he thinks of Washington lawyers if for no reason other than propinquity.

There have, however, been countervailing trends. The federal district courts have been vested by the Tucker Act with concurrent jurisdiction over certain types of claims against the United States. Court of Claims Commissioners hold hearings away from Washington and have commanded, by the high level of their abilities, such a regard for their proposed findings of fact, that one might properly call the five-man bench in Washington a court of appeal for a large number of roving trial courts. Despite these factors, however, there still remains, in Washington, a limited and identifiable group of individuals that can properly be called a Court of Claims bar.

The United States Tax Court stands on a different footing. It has an imperfect situs in Washington, for its judges, unlike those of the Court of Claims, hold hearings away from Washington. True, practice before the Tax Court is largely confined to tax lawyers, and in that sense it has a bar of its own, in Washington as well as in every city in the United States. My feeling, however, is that this is different, in that the court has not created a bar to serve it, but rather has served as the judicial agency for a segment of law practice which was fairly well-defined before the Tax Court was created.

The Court of Customs and Patent Appeals, also a Washington institution, is of the same type – that is, it came into existence, as to customs appeals in 1910 and as to patent appeals in 1929, to meet the judicial needs of already specialized segments of the legal profession. On its customs side, it has a bar, but one which practices before the Customs Court in New York and other major ports of entry, and which is almost entirely unrepresented in Washington. Patent, trade-mark and copyright lawyers, as I have already observed, no longer feel the need of propinquity to the Patent Office, and the early predominance of the Washington patent and trade-mark bar has been forced to yield, in large measure, to the patent and trade-mark firms of other cities.

There remains for discussion the relationship of the Washington lawyer to the regular courts of the District of Columbia. Almost by definition, if you will, he is rarely an attorney in the lower levels of the local judicial hierarchy – the Municipal Court and the Municipal Court of Appeals. In the District Court, however, and in the United States Court of Appeals, he may well appear frequently. Both courts have a dual jurisdiction. They are, on the one hand, the regular courts for all matters which pertain to the private affairs of the citizens of Washington — divorce, wills, torts, local crimes, contracts, corporation law, and the like. On such matters, the United States Court of Appeals stands in substantially the same position as, say, the Supreme Court of Illinois.

On the other hand, the District Court and the Court of Appeals are regular federal courts, equivalent to the United States District Court for the Northern District of Illinois and the Court of Appeals for the Seventh Circuit. It is with this aspect of their work — perhaps 10 per cent of the cases in the District Court and something over 30 per cent of the cases in the Court of Appeals — that the Washington lawyer may be concerned.

That is not to say that there is a bar which specializes in this part of the practice before these courts. I rather think it cannot be fairly described that way, since the practitioners are largely those Washington lawyers who are engaged in the several types of administrative practice which we will examine later, and who find it necessary to challenge in court the decisions of the executive or administrative branch. A sampling of cases would show that on occasion relief is sought in the District Court, usually by way of writs of mandamus or injunction, against officials or bodies such as the Attorney General, the Secretary of the Army or the Secretary of Defense, the Housing Expediter, the Veterans' Administrator, the Board of Immigration Appeals, the Commissioner of Patents, and the Maritime Administration, all of which are located in, or at least can be served with process in, the District of Columbia.

The Court of Appeals has, in addition to appellate review of District Court matters, far more than a normal share of petitions to review orders of federal regulatory agencies. Congress has usually provided that the Court of Appeals for the District of Columbia is a jurisdiction alternate to the Court of Appeals in the area where the affected person resides or has his principal place of business. Apart from petitions to review orders of the National Labor Relations Board, which are distributed quite generally among the circuits, more petitions to review agency orders are filed in the Court of Appeals for the District of Columbia than in all other Courts of Appeals combined.[10] It is fair to say that this is not entirely due to the special competence and experience of the local Court of Appeals, and its convenience to local lawyers.

Before we leave the subject of the Washington lawyer's relation to the judiciary, one general comment is warranted. Washington lawyers are peculiarly ubiquitous. Representing as they do clients everywhere in the United States who have federal problems, Washington lawyers must be able to pack their brief cases and speed anywhere to do battle with the Department of Justice, or the tax collector, or the Office of Price Stabilization. A Washington firm with considerable litigation may find its partners in New York, or Chicago, or San Francisco, or anywhere in the United States – probably more frequently than it finds them in Washington. The life of a litigating Washington lawyer is a peripatetic one, and if he is an antitrust lawyer, who measures the length of his trials in months, or even years, his family is open to the conviction that he really is not a lawyer in Washington at all.

The responsibilities of representing nation-wide clients are almost equally demanding on those whose trial practice is nil. The long-distance telephone call is no substitute for a conference. Travel – although not in antitrust doses – is so routine that for many lawyers presence in Washington for a full calendar week is the event which evokes comment.

No one professes to enjoy it; no one knows how to avoid it.

Let us now turn to the Washington lawyer in his relation to the second major branch of the federal government — the legislative. Principally, this will have to do with lobbying — using the term in the broad sense of activity intended to influence legislative action. At the outset, however, it is worth noting that lobbying is not the only work for the Washington lawyer in the legislative field.

Washington has always had a full share of litigation challenging the powers of Congress and of congressional committees. Contempt of Congress and perjury cases are not unique to investigations of Communism, interstate crime, or tax frauds. The famous early contempt cases known in their day as the *Sugar Trust Cases* [11] and the even earlier proceedings in *Kilbourn* v. *Thompson* [12] were both tried out in the local courts. Advice to clients on when they should testify and when they may properly claim privilege has been sought and given for over a century.

Moreover, still apart from anything which can properly be called lobbying, there is what might be called the Washington lawyer's interpretation and evaluation work. A bill is introduced which, on its face, means nothing; let us say that it reads like this: "The fourth proviso of subsection (b) of Section 1 of the Act of March 2, 1937, is amended by deleting the words following the word 'assessment,' and changing the comma which follows said word to a semi-colon." The lawyer who has undertaken to advise a client on legislative developments will have a preliminary interpretation job. Likewise, in a bill which proposes new language in place of old, the lawyer will have to evaluate the potential effect of the bill in terms of how radically it breaks with the past. If the client happens to be one which does considerable business with the government, not only substantive bills but appropriation bills must be analyzed and evaluated. The process of reporting, interpreting and evaluating continues through the several legislative stages – the hearings, the committee reports, the floor debates.

At first blush, there seems to be nothing in this which calls for any particular qualifications except an access to the bills and reports. For the Washington lawyer they are conveniently at hand, but they are available in due course to lawyers everywhere. Speed, however, is often important, or at least many clients so regard it. More importantly, the evaluation of proposed legislation demands a considerable understanding of the prevailing political moods of individual Senators and Congressmen, of congressional committees, and of Congress as a whole. Lawmaking is a political process, and political factors are as important as legal ones. Not all bills are significant – they range from those which represent the individual aberrations of a single member or a small pressure group to so-called administration "must" bills. At either extreme they are easily identified; the skill lies in assigning a fair position on the scale to those which fall somewhere in between. Committee clerks, individual members of Congress, officials in the executive branch, and many others all supply general information, background, "feel" for the answer.

Recognizing, then, that the Washington lawyer has functions in connection with the legislative process which have no external impact, let us turn to the role of the Washington lawyer in lobbying – in activity intended to influence legislation. Probably that is his chief role in the legislative function.

Do not let this statement be a shock. I use the words "lobbying" and "lobbyist" as neutral words –

in the same sense as they are used, for example, in the Federal Regulation of Lobbying Act. In that sense, they are convenient words, and I believe we will come to a better understanding of the activities of the Washington lawyer if we can put behind us the unsavory overtones which "lobbyist" has historically borne. Walt Whitman inveighed against "bawling office holders . . . kept editors . . . bribers, compromisers, lobbiers, spongers . . . the lousy combings and born freedom-sellers of the earth." Even now, for the politician, Senator James Reed of Missouri has given what is probably the permanent definition: "A lobbyist is anyone who opposes legislation I want."

All political campaigns in the past have evoked a full share of condemnation of this or that "lobby." Yet I suggest that a much more realistic statement is that of the most recent congressional committee investigating the subject:

> Every democratic society worthy of the name must have some lawful means by which individuals and groups can lay their needs before government. One of the central purposes of government is that people should be able to reach it . . . with maximum impact and possibility of success. This is, fundamentally what lobbying is about.[13]

It is in that sense that I propose to use the term.

Let me make clear, however, that when I use "lobbying" as a neutral word, I do not mean to ignore all the political imponderables which are wrapped up in representative government. Lobbying, it can be said, necessarily means "pressure" government, in which the interests of the public get lost in the shuffle. There is real basis for doubt whether we can presently accept the answer of Madison, advanced in *The Federalist*, that the aggressive forces in American life will neutralize each other.

Whether that criticism is sound is not a matter within the scope of this book. Let us recognize that there is a problem when we have a group which is in the minority but which has an intensity of feeling, a complete understanding of what may be a complex issue, and adequate funds. Such a group may be able to impose its desires on a complacent, uninformed majority. There is no accurate gauge which can be applied to distinguish, as the *New York Times* has put it, "between a million dollars and a million votes." And Congress will always have the problem of recognizing the distinction between situations where countervailing pressures clearly exist, as in the recent butter-margarine controversy, and situations where all the pressures are likely to be on one side, as in a tariff act, or in a bill appropriating money for public works.

Using the term "lobbying" in a neutral sense will not resolve these problems. It means simply that I do not propose to use the term as synonymous with its abuses – bribery, direct or indirect, fake letters or telegrams, influence-peddling, and the like. To me these are no more characteristic of lobbying than is bribery of jurors or use of manufactured evidence characteristic of trial practice.

From the point of view of the Washington lawyer, there are two types of lobbying which we can promptly eliminate from discussion. First, there are activities directed at influencing legislation through the electoral process – that is, by supporting the election to the legislative body of a person with a legislative program one favors. Second, there are activities directed at influencing legislation by "educational work." If you happen to oppose the particular legislative action which is in issue, substitute for the phrase "educational work" the phrase "propaganda work." The education or propaganda may be specific, directed toward a particular bill, or it may be directed only at the establishment of a political or economic philosophy which will condition all future legislation. This latter has been called "grass roots" lobbying. The Washington lawyer, like any other citizen, may participate in both of these types of lobbying activities, but neither category has any special relation to either his location or his skills.

The other two kinds of lobbying, with which the Washington lawyer is concerned, are of a more direct sort. The first is the most direct – contacts or communications with specific legislators or legislative committees. The other is the contact with an interested government department or agency to secure its approval and cooperation in presenting and securing the passage of a bill. In each of these fields, the special competence of the lawyer is both used and useful.

This, of course, is not a new function. Lobbying in the broad sense is as old as representative government itself. There are a number of factors, however, which suggest that it is more important now than it was a century ago. It is true that one prolific field for lobbying has been substantially decreased – the field of private bills by which individuals seek legislative relief. The creation of the

Court of Claims during the Civil War, and the renunciation to it of contractual and quasi-contractual claims for relief against the government, diverted some of the flood. The recent Federal Tort Claims Act of 1946, by which still more jurisdiction was ceded to the federal courts, has substantially relieved the judiciary committees, at least, of this burden. There are still private bills by the hundreds, for which lobbying may be essential, in which individuals seek legislative relief beyond the powers, or even against the judgments, of the courts, but the crest of the flood has passed.

The decrease of opportunities for lobbying in that direction, however, is more than offset by the increased number of clients who seek help in connection with the growth of the federal government and its impact on the business community. As early as 1850, we find the United States Brewers' Association was formed with the explanation that "owners of breweries, separately, are unable to exercise a proper influence on the legislature and public administration." No doubt many trade associations, as well as the large groups representing the entire business community such as the National Association of Manufacturers and the United States Chamber of Commerce, may have had among their founding purposes a drive to stand for or against legislative action, state as well as federal. Moreover, *ad hoc,* temporary pressure groups have come and gone with increasing frequency in recent years.

But without speculating further on how much lobby work there is now and whether it is increasing or decreasing, let us see if we can form a basis for some conclusion on the Washington lawyer's participation in it, by examining certain concrete types of legal work designed to influence legislative action. First, let us take a sample of what is a frequent occurrence – the drafting of proposed legislation. Here there are perhaps three skills of the lawyer which are involved – the ability to write, in the sense of using words exactly and intelligibly; the appreciation, in that writing, of secondary or particular meanings of words in specific legal contexts; and finally the appreciation and wise choice of approach to a legislative solution, taking into account not only political imponderables, but also the relationship of the proposed act to other statutes, or even to the Constitution itself.

These important political imponderables are the basis for some interesting statutory clauses. For example, when the Price Control Extension Act of 1946 [14] was in process of being drafted, there was no doubt that agricultural commodities would be given a particularly favorable position. The solemn pronouncement in Section 7 of that Act that "fish and other sea foods shall be deemed to be agricultural commodities" is an illustration of sagacious draftsmanship, not of haste or ignorance.

Another recent example of the need for high legal skills, is the Portal-to-Portal Act of 1947.[15] The Supreme Court, in *Anderson* v. *Mt. Clemens Pottery Co.*,[16] had ruled that certain preliminary and postliminary activities of employees — which were loosely called "travel time" — constituted time worked under the Fair Labor Standards Act. Earlier decisions had already made clear that the statutory liability for overtime pay could neither be compromised by the employer nor avoided by the courts.[17] Industry was faced with a liability for back overtime pay estimated at over five billion dollars. Legislation was the only avenue of relief.

No doubt many clients, alarmed by their own potential liability, and concerned that legislative relief be both promptly forthcoming and effective when it arrived, requested Washington lawyers to draft a bill to be submitted to their Congressman or Senator, or presented at committee hearings.

The first question was a vital one: Which approach had the best chance of surmounting the obvious constitutional questions suggested by the necessarily retroactive character of the legislation? Lawyers explored the possibility of a legislative declaration that these preliminary and postliminary activities were *de minimis;* of a repeal of the Act retroactively with a new definition of "work" in the re-enactment; of a 95 or 100 per cent tax on the proceeds of any successful suit; of the withdrawal of jurisdiction from the courts to entertain suits for back overtime pay; and of other, and even more esoteric procedures.

Once there was a determination of this issue — and it is an indication of its difficulty that judgments varied widely — the lawyer proceeded to draft proposed sections of the bill. Usually, a memorandum was also prepared, to be submitted with the draft of the bill, partly to convince Congress that it did have power to give effective relief, and partly to convince it of the best way to exercise this power. Both the proposed language for the bill, and the memorandum, were finally submitted to individual Senators and Congressmen, or to the committee for inclusion in the record of the committee hearings.

In major bills, such as this proposed amendment to the Fair Labor Standards Act, it is fair to say that private assistance in draftsmanship is usually unnecessary. In such cases, and indeed in most legislation, Congress has had since 1918, and has utilized, the drafting services of the Office of the Legislative Counsel – a title which itself recognizes the legal nature of the work.[18] The Office frees the Congress from the necessity of relying solely upon private parties or the executive agencies of the government, but, as in the case we have just noted, does not remove either the propriety or in some cases the necessity for private parties to present their own views on problems of draftsmanship or policy.

Let us take another example, somewhat more removed from the direct contact with Congress, but nonetheless lobbying, as we have defined it – that is, activity intended to affect legislative action. This one, as it happens, has its whole background stated in the public record.[19] The salmon canners in Alaska for many years had been engaged in a controversy with the Alaskan Indians and the Department of the Interior concerning the respective rights of the canners and the Indians to fish in certain Alaskan waters. The problem was most acute in respect to fish traps — large, fixed nets — which the canners and others had for many years maintained at strategic locations. The Indian tribes wanted fish traps too, but most of the available locations, or at least most of the best ones, were already pre-empted.

The canners proposed to resolve the controversy by legislation rather than litigation. Being politically practical, however, they recognized that without Department of Interior approval, no legislation would be likely to pass, so they sought the aid of Washington counsel in drafting a bill which would secure that approval and support when it was presented to Congress. Here, the lawyer's problem was partly legal — Indian rights in Alaska are a veritable legal nightmare — but principally the work was practical — how to balance the conflicting equities of the canners and the Indian tribes in order that they both might be more legally secure. Drafts were prepared. Many conferences were held with many Department of Interior officials — its Solicitor, representatives of its Fish and Wildlife and Indian Affairs Divisions, an Assistant Secretary and the Secretary himself. The proposed bill was drafted and redrafted and redrafted. Agreement finally was reached, and the bill was finally introduced at the request of the Department.

This once-removed-from-Congress lobbying is far more usual than might appear. Bills considered by Congress – even private bills – almost always deal with a matter which is of direct concern to some federal department or agency, and they are generally referred to that agency as a matter of course by the congressional committees. Experience teaches that seldom, if ever, does a bill slip by without the agency making its views known – by appearance in a hearing, if the bill gets that far, or by a letter to the committee which may end its legislative flight before it ever gets off the ground. Common prudence dictates, therefore, that before serious attempts are made to secure any legislative action, conferences with the interested government officials are desirable. Perhaps the lawyer's efforts are so fully successful that the bill will be proposed as a government measure. And even though there is usually not a complete agreement, by compromise or otherwise, such as in my fish-trap illustration, at least some areas of disagreement are eliminated, non-significant matters can be reconciled, and the later hearings focused on the critical issues.

A frequent illustration of this type of legislative activity is in the field of taxation. Here, all would admit, draftsmanship of a high order must be combined with a thorough understanding of related provisions and the applicable judicial precedents. Congress has itself recognized the problems by the creation of a Joint Committee on Internal Revenue Taxation, with a corps of legal, technical and clerical assistants headed by a Chief of Staff who is probably without an equal in thorough understanding of federal taxes. Because this committee exists, the approach of the Washington lawyer in this field combines both the departmental approach with the direct contact with a congressional committee.

A lawyer who seeks a change in a provision of the tax law, or who, perchance, wishes to avoid a change in a particular tax provision, will usually start with the office of the Tax Legislative Counsel in the General Counsel's Office of the Treasury Department. There are situations, however – and it is a part of expertise to recognize them – where the initial approach will be with the Chief Counsel of the Bureau of Internal Revenue. By memoranda and personal conferences on the merits of the change, or, if no change is wanted, on the merits of the present law, the lawyer will attempt to persuade the Department to accept and incorporate the lawyer's position in its tax recommendations to Congress. Memoranda and arguments are not only legal, but economic, sociological, and political; in short, in many cases they will include the same material as the departmental staff itself would prepare for the Secretary of the Treasury on the same topic. Where the Treasury is known to have a different point of view from that which the lawyer urges, the memoranda and arguments will of course attempt to meet it.

In the field of taxes, however, Congress has many ideas of its own which may be quite opposed to those of the Treasury, and for which it relies on the technical services of the staff of the Joint Committee, supplemented by information from the Treasury Department. In such an area – and again it is part of expertise to know where those areas lie – the contacts will begin with that staff, which will be consulted, argued with, and perhaps persuaded to act, or to refrain from acting. Indeed, it is one of the functions of that staff to evaluate and correlate proposals for changes in the tax law from whatever source. To the extent that the Washington lawyer can be of practical assistance to the staff, in preparing an accurate and helpful evaluation and analysis of the tax provisions in which the lawyer is interested, just to that extent may the lawyer expect that he will advantage his client's position. At this level, at least – whatever may be the determinative factors which operate at the congressional committee and floor debate stages – the decisions are almost entirely on the tax merits of the proposal, and a good brief in support of a position is as helpful as it is in a court. And let me repeat it, such activity is not confined to attempts to introduce affirmative changes; tax provisions which are helpful to your clients may equally require effort to keep them in the law.

Let us admit, however, that what we have been talking about thus far is the unusual rather than the usual type of a Washington lawyer's congressional activity. Much more common is the client who is affected by a bill with which he has had nothing to do until it is introduced. Laws being what they are and clients being what they are, more than likely the client wishes that he had never heard of it. What such a client wants is to oppose, or perhaps to favor, that bill. Why does he come to a Washington lawyer?

There are several possibilities. He may wish the lawyer to testify for him. The lawyer, being aware of the fact that on Capitol Hill one constituent is worth a platoon of lawyers, will discourage that proposal, though there are cases in which it is appropriate. A simple example will suffice. An association of government employees had persuaded the department in which they worked that the special law under which their overtime was computed was in need of substantial revision in the light of recent court decisions construing it. A bill had already been introduced and was pending before a subcommittee of the House Committee on Ways and Means. The president of the employees' association was competent to testify on the merits of the overtime system, and did so, but he requested his Washington lawyer also to appear and testify on the legal developments which had provoked the bill. The client might have been served by the filing of a memorandum; actually, the legal issues were quite complex, and well worth an oral presentation at which questions could be asked and answered.

In that case, there was no necessity for the lawyer

to assist his client in the presentation of the practical aspects of the case. He was highly intelligent, he was vocal, and he knew his subject from intimate daily experience. In many cases, that is not the case. A client may arrive in your office, anxious to oppose or favor a bill. Hearings may have been set, and he wants to appear, and wants you to help him to get ready. There is work for you to do.

Conversation will bring out, painfully or promptly as the case may be, why he takes the position he does, and a general flavor of the reasons he can advance. You are then in a position at once similar to but at the same time very different from that of a lawyer preparing a witness for a trial. True, you don't have to worry about the rules of evidence, but you become more keenly aware of the fact that opinion evidence and sweeping conclusions and generalizations are poor substitutes for carefully circumscribed and documented statements, charts and graphs. You also know that even though you need not fear greatly that irrelevant material will be excluded, your witness will have only a limited amount of time in which to present a position, and time spent on irrelevancies is simply time wasted. You explore the possibility of reasons other than the ones your client has thought of. You imagine all possible arguments on the other side, and determine which ones to try to meet, which ones to ignore, and which ones to try to skate over lightly. And when all of that is done, you make sure that your client understands what you have prepared, agrees with it, and can answer – you hope – such questions as the committee may put to him.

The differences from a judicial proceeding are fundamental in that the issues are always, in the large sense, political. Potential witnesses must be evaluated in terms of at least the states represented by the members of the committee. Members of Congress are not unnaturally interested in what their own constituents have to say. Perhaps such a witness is desirable even if he is not as fully qualified on the merits as you would like; you still need the tangible evidence of his interest and support. Again, the lawyer will attempt to develop, as a political device, a "polar" phrase – "retroactive laws are bad," "natural resources must be conserved," "small business," "injury to competition," "American system of free enterprise," or the like, which can be repeated and repeated. In short, the motivating factors for a member of Congress are not only the intrinsic merits of a proposal, but also its political implications, and neither can be ignored.

Such assignments for a Washington lawyer are frequent. When he himself is to be the witness, or when he is simply to prepare a written statement to be submitted "for the record," the work will be essentially the same, though perhaps a little less nerve-wracking and time-consuming.

Thus far, we would no doubt all agree that the Washington lawyer is largely exercising the normal skills and abilities of the profession – draftsmanship, marshaling of facts, distillation of issues and arguments as well as resolution of purely legal issues. Let us pursue his activities into areas where his work may be less directly legal. Either in connection with some of the activities already described, or independent of them, a Washington lawyer may be brought directly into legislative activity. Let us say that on some particular measure in which a client is interested the lines have begun to be drawn in Congress. Some of the members are known to be on the client's side. Others are doubtful. The lawyer visits, and seeks to persuade, the doubtful ones who are important, using, let us assume for the moment – to avoid a problem we must face later –

the same sort of arguments he has made, or would have made, in a public hearing. Perhaps he may put the essential facts and arguments into a memorandum which can be distributed to many members of Congress.

With a member of Congress who is already on the client's side, the lawyer offers or suggests that he may be of additional help. Perhaps he can prepare helpful questions, or lines of questions, that may be asked during the committee hearings. Possibly he can be useful in composing the committee report. Or, assuming that the bill has reached the floor of either house, he may assist a member of Congress in preparing a speech for their common position. Members of Congress are notoriously overworked, and the lawyer may have the time and the facilities which the member lacks to analyze the record made at the hearings, or to summarize the arguments, or to suggest new ones. If the bill as it emerges from the committees is not entirely clear, and the lawyer can foresee future arguments in the Supreme Court on its proper construction, there may be substantial advantages to the client in suggestions on how the intent of the Congress might be clarified – by speeches which might be made, or by amendments which might be proposed and discussed even if they may ultimately be defeated, or by the sort of legislative cross-examination which smokes out the real purpose of the proposed law through carefully drawn questions addressed to the chairman of the committee which reported the bill, or to its principal proponent in the floor debate.

There is a basic distinction between activities of this sort and those in my prior examples – here the lawyer is not working "on the record." His work is not secret, but it may never come to public attention. On the other hand, there is – or let us be more cautious and say that we will, for the purpose of the discussion at this point, assume that there is – a similarity, in that the lawyer is still concerning himself with the merits of the matter at issue.

No doubt the non-public nature of this sort of lawyer's work lends itself to the ready suspicion that it is not legal work at all, but influence-peddling or worse. But let us stick to our assumption, and try to see whether a line can or should be drawn between the proper and the improper in relation to what we have thus far described.

The direct guide is none too helpful. Canon 26

of the Canons of Professional Ethics of the American Bar Association reads as follows:

> A lawyer openly, and in his true character, may render professional services before legislative or other bodies, regarding proposed legislation and in advocacy of claims before departments of government, upon the same principles of ethics which justify his appearance before the Courts; but it is unprofessional for a lawyer so engaged to conceal his attorneyship or to employ secret personal solicitations, or to use means other than those addressed to the reason and understanding, to influence action.

This Canon has had no pertinent official interpretation.

Let us leave until later the application of the canon to advocacy of claims before the government departments and now look at its application to lobbying. One matter is clear: an attorney who engages in any of the activities we have described, cannot, with propriety, conceal his attorneyship. This is plainly and rightfully condemned. But there clarity ends. What is the significance of the phrase in the first section of the Canon that the lawyer may render professional services "before legislative . . . bodies"? Does the reference to "bodies" mean to exclude all contact with the individual member of Congress? To state the extreme case, does it mean that a client cannot with propriety request his Washington lawyer to accompany him in his attempt to persuade his own Congressman or Senator to introduce a bill which he has drafted? And does it mean that only at the risk of being accused of unprofessional conduct may a Washington lawyer visit an individual member of Congress for discussion of the merits of a bill?

We get no help from the second "thou shalt not" section of the Canon. Its clauses are in the disjunctive, and there is an unqualified ban on "secret personal solicitations." Does "secret" mean to prohibit everything except appearances before committees? Specifically, does it prohibit a discussion with a member of Congress in his office, at which the lawyer attempts to persuade him by reasoned arguments? Does the word "personal" in the phrase "secret personal solicitations" mean that it bans only those non-public contacts where personal influence or favors, and not the merits, are the basis of the appeal?

The latter interpretation certainly sounds more reasonable, but if it is to be accepted it means that the whole clause simply duplicates the clause which immediately follows it — that no means shall be used "other than those addressed to the reason and understanding." For that matter, what does that mean? Literally, it means that a lawyer must close his eyes to the fact that lawmaking is a political process — unless "reason and understanding" implies that a lawyer may attempt to make clear to the members of Congress the political facts of life.

In truth, the Canon is either so strict as to be impossible, or so vague as to be useless. Washington lawyers do all of these things, and in my opinion properly so. Both the public and the non-public aspects of such work call for his legal abilities, and for the wisdom, understanding and judgment that can come only from experience in many cases, many victories and defeats, over many years.

The reader is no doubt saying to himself — all this is very well, but in view of the daily press, is it not more to the point that you speak of the improprieties than of the proprieties? My excuse, which I hope is recognized, is that it is important to know what Washington lawyers do, and to know that there are manifold ways in which they can properly engage in activities designed to affect legislation — can lobby, as we use the term. Perhaps I make my bow to the current state of public opinion in acknowledging that such a proposition requires exposition.

Certainly, I cannot vouch for the ethical standards among Washington lawyer-lobbyists. I think they are generally high, and that the principal criticism of lobbying activities is in fact directed at the non-lawyer lobbyists, who outnumber the lawyers perhaps ten to one. But neither do I challenge the assertion that there are, and will be, lawyers who recognize no limits. Vague as the ethical standards may be, there is clearly a line that no lawyer should pass. Fundamentally, there can be no more basis for a lawyer to obtain the vote of a member of Congress on the basis of friendship, or on the basis of past, present or future favors, than there is for a lawyer to obtain a vote from a judge or a juror on the same basis. The lawyer stands on a different footing from his client. John Smith, the voter, and also the man who favors H.R. 10,000, can with propriety tell his Congressman that the price of Smith's next vote or his next campaign contribution is the Congressman's own vote for H.R. 10,000. It may be poor citizenship; it may move the Congressman to vote against, rather than for, H.R. 10,000. But it is the essence of democracy, it seems to me, that voters should be able to tell a member of Congress what they want, and to tell the member that if he disagrees, he will lose that voter's support in the next campaign.

The Washington lawyer, or any other lawyer, for that matter, is not the voter. He is retained, and paid, for professional advice and services. But when he is retained, or paid, for his influence or alleged influence over a member of Congress, regardless of the merits of the issue, he is no longer acting as a lawyer.

This is summary treatment of a complex and controversial part of the mechanics of democratic government. Later there will be occasion to treat it in a little more detail, and from a different point of view. Probably, however, no matter how much is said, there are always more problems raised than answered. This chapter will have served its purpose if it was done no more than paint a general background into which we can later fit a few more problems, and into which there can be fitted, as understanding grows, the forever unfolding stories of events along the Potomac.

II. Activities Relating to the Executive Branch and the Administrative Agencies

IN CHAPTER I we completed an examination of the first two aspects of the Washington lawyer's work – his activities in connection with the courts, and his activities in connection with Congress. There remains the third aspect – his work in connection with the federal administrative agencies and the executive branch of the federal government.

Although this is unquestionably the Washington lawyer's major field of activity, it is also the most difficult to impound. Partly this is true because the diversity of activity is so pronounced that generalization and synthesis tend to be unrealistic and unrewarding. What is generally encompassed in the phrase "administrative law practice" is a seamless web, and to speak about any of its particular characteristics tends to give an undue emphasis and hence a distorted picture. Nor is there either pleasure or profit in the recitation of a series of specific incidents or idiosyncrasies.

Before we attempt to describe present-day administrative law practice, however, we can profitably spend a few minutes looking backwards. We have enough history for a perspective. With a perspective we can see more clearly some of the reasons why administrative agencies are so various and so amorphous, and we can better appreciate some of the facets of administrative practice which make it both a high art and a headache. One author has commented:

> . . . A hundred years ago, it must be remembered, human affairs in peacetime were largely entrusted to three ancient, if not equally honored, professions – the doctor, to cope with bodily ills; the minister, to deal with those of the soul against the day of inevitable failure of the doctor; and the lawyer, to deal with all other professional needs. To a large extent, only the lawyer presumed to practice the arts of government in the legislature or in the courts where rules of conduct were hammered out on the anvil of litigation. The administrative process, either of rule-making or adjudication, was virtually unknown; and the invidious connotations of the term "bureaucrat" were still undeveloped.[1]

This does not mean, of course, that administrative agencies are entirely a recent invention. The Attorney General's Committee on Administrative Procedure noted [2] that the administrative concept traces back to 1789, and that numerous agencies were originated prior to 1933. But merely to tabulate the several years in which administrative agencies came into existence does not give a true picture. To say, for example, that the Bureau of Internal Revenue dates back to 1862 does not take into account the fact that the present agency which bears that name is so different in size and complexity of function as to be an entirely different agency.

The real beginnings of the modern administrative process probably can be put in the first administration of Woodrow Wilson. During that period, Congress created, for example, the Federal Trade Commission and the Federal Reserve Board, established the Labor Department, and imposed new limitations on business activity by the Clayton Act. The full flowering, however, occurred in the 1930's, with the flood of alphabetical agencies, all of them administrative, and almost all endowed with wide discretion and broad rule-making power. And not only did Congress create new agencies; it also conferred broad and important new powers on established ones through such statutes as the Fair Labor Standards Act, the Robinson-Patman Act, and the Food, Drug and Cosmetic Act of 1938. Moreover, expanding constitutional concepts of interstate commerce brought large segments of the economy under regulation for the first time.

The feature of this administrative growth and development which makes generalization so difficult is that agencies and agency powers did not come into being as a result of theoretical speculation about the ideal structure of government. Speculation and rationalization came later, as men sought to explain where this new "art form" of government had come from. By and large, each agency owed its existence to an attempt by Congress – and latterly by the Executive – to solve some concrete problem. Sometimes the purpose was to regulate, and there was created an Interstate Commerce Commission, or a Federal Maritime Board, or, in times of emergency, agencies such as the National Production Authority or the Office of Price Stabilization. At other times, the purpose was to perform services or confer benefits, which gave us agencies such as the Export-Import Bank, the Rural Electrification Administration, the Home Owners' Loan Corporation, and the Bureau of Indian Affairs. There are many other familiar categories. We may even have regulation of the regulators, such as is done by that agency which masquerades under the deceptive title of the Bureau of the Budget, and, in the field of the government's own housekeeping, by the General Services Administration.

Nor were the purposes always unitary. Crop loans to farmers represent economic aid, but they also have an important regulatory purpose. The Tennessee Valley Authority is certainly something more than a power project. The National Labor Relations Act and the Fair Labor Standards Act were not concerned entirely with securing the free flow of interstate commerce. Whatever the purpose or purposes, however, one inevitable result was new subject matter requiring the attention of the Washington lawyer.

Because the starting point in every instance has been a problem rather than a theory, the organization and operation of different agencies reflects no symmetry, but rather an endless diversity of forms. The power conferred might be rule-making, or licensing, or adjudication, or it might be a combination of all three. To these were usually added powers to investigate, prosecute or negotiate. Each particular permutation presents its own problems.

Before we approach those problems, however, let us examine the reaction of the bar to this new form of government. Lawyers generally have only in recent decades become aware that there was such a thing as an administrative process. First awareness, for many, was not a pleasant one. Rare indeed have been the major administrative agencies which did not become the subject of heated controversy. There were some among the lawyers who sought calmly to study and understand the new development. For the most part, however, the division of legal opinion was between those who attacked, and even abused and vilified, and those who blindly defended and unqualifiedly praised.

In part, the extreme viewpoints can be attributed to disagreement over the substantive policies to which the new processes were tied. Moreover, the procedures were new, and therefore strange. They were in large measure experimental, and therefore fumbling and faulty. It was natural that some should see great promise, and others grave dangers. Nevertheless, it comes as something of a shock today to see the bitterness implicit in a caution which John Foster Dulles found it necessary to give lawyers as late as 1939:

The lawyer dealing with a commission should not carry into his work prejudices and resentment which are perhaps natural but which, in justice to the client, must not be allowed to color the lawyer's judgment and action. He should, for example, be very sure that he does not unwittingly encourage the client to fight a commission because this will afford the lawyer a chance to vent his general feelings against commissions as such.[3]

Throughout the furor over theories of government and the wisdom of specific practices, the prophecy and advice of Elihu Root, given as early as 1916, proved to be very true:

. . . We are entering upon the creation of a body of administrative law quite different in its machinery, its remedies, and its necessary safeguards from the old methods of regulation by specific statutes enforced by the courts. As any community passes from simple to complex conditions the only way in which government can deal with the increased burdens thrown upon it is by the delegation of power to be exercised in detail by subordinate agents, subject to the control of general directions prescribed by superior authority. The necessities of our situation have already led to an extensive employment of that method. . . . Before these agencies the old doctrine prohibiting the delegation of legislative power has virtually retired from the field and given up the fight. There will be no withdrawal from these experiments. We shall go on; we shall expand them, whether we approve theoretically or not, because such agencies furnish protection to rights and obstacles to wrongdoing which under our new social and industrial conditions cannot be practically accomplished by the old and simple procedure of legislatures and courts as in the last generation. Yet the powers that are committed to those regulatory agencies, and which they must have to do their work, carry with them great and dangerous opportunities of oppression and wrong. If we are to continue a government of limited powers, these agencies of regulation must themselves be regulated. The limits of their power over the citizen must be fixed and determined. The rights of the citizen against them must be made plain. A system of administrative law must be developed . . .[4]

With the passage of the Administrative Procedure Act in 1946, the bitterness of controversy appears to have subsided, though it has not disappeared. Perhaps it would be more accurate to say that controversy over administrative law has been replaced by controversy over the Administrative Procedure Act. Yet despite the deficiencies of that Act, it is gradually teaching administrators in the agencies that they can operate, and operate effectively, despite limited procedural restraints. Lawyers, too, have learned that it is possible to live with these new bodies of government, although they are still very much in the process of discovering how best to do it.

But now let us turn from history. To get at our particular problem, let us take up some of the salient characteristics of administrative agencies, and consider how these have in turn influenced the characteristics of Washington law practice. That they have had an impact should occasion no surprise, but the manner is of some interest.

Of all the features which are sufficiently common to a number of agencies to warrant calling them characteristics, I have arbitrarily selected three. They may not be the three most important; they shade off into each other; and they are not universally applicable; but they appear to be sufficiently definite and important to deserve special attention.

First, then, let us examine some of the effects on the Washington lawyer of what is probably the basic characteristic of administrative agencies — their broad delegation of power to intervene actively in private affairs. This characteristic is, perhaps, a function of the new concept of preventive law, coupled with an almost total abandonment of constitutional limits on delegation of authority. This combination has led one lawyer to describe agencies as "a weapon which is like a flaming sword" as compared to judicially enforced statutes of earlier days.[5] Another has said: "For clean-cut law with police enforcement there has been substituted a value judgment, with an agency designed for continuous intervention in the realization of this value."[6] This is emphatically a government of men, not of laws; a kinetic force which permeates every aspect of business, and encroaches more and more on our personal lives. But it has been growing rather than lessening, and the lawyer's job has been to adjust to it.

One consequence, the significance of which is perhaps not generally realized, is the extent to which the lawyer has been required to enter more and more into active participation in administrative proceedings. For the business lawyer, during the nineteenth century and even into the early decades of the twentieth, there was a pronounced decline in advocacy, and a pronounced increase in counseling and advisory work. Elihu Root could truthfully remark: "Of course a lawyer's chief business is to keep his clients out of litigation."[7] So long as the prevailing mode of regulation was by statutes enforceable only by prosecutions and penalties, a lawyer could reasonably hope that if the client were willing to seek legal advice, controversy with the government, at least, could be confined to matters where the advice was bad, or where the answer was doubtful and the decision was deliberately made to accept the legal risks.

Modern administrative law, for the Washington lawyer, has restored advocacy to a significant place. No amount of prophylactic counseling can avoid administrative hearings and controversies. New laws in the form of regulations and rules are being proposed every day, and only vigorous and continued participation in the lawmaking process by the Washington lawyer will adequately protect his clients' interests.

Many examples come readily to mind. The statute which outlaws "misbranded" foods now confers upon the Food and Drug Administration the power to hold hearings and issue regulations defining the components of a lawful food product. The lawyer's job is no longer simply how to advise his client on how best to avoid the stigma of misbranding. A Washington lawyer who represents a baker, for example, cannot emulate Mr. Root, or he may discover that a particular kind of bread which his client is successfully marketing can no longer be legally sold as bread, or even legally sold at all. Not only the baker, but also those who supply the ingredients for his product, will insist that counsel attend the hearings and protect their interests. Again, to take the somewhat different example of a regulated industry, while counseling is important, on major matters such as the merger of two airlines or the acquisition of a radio station or the abandonment of a railroad line, all the preliminary counseling in the world cannot avoid the likelihood of an administrative hearing where the proposal must be defended.

This may be advocacy of a different sort than that of the courtroom, to be sure; indeed, it is far closer to the work of the lawyer before committees of Congress. Nor do I mean that counseling has become outmoded. It certainly remains of great importance, and later I shall discuss it further. But with the bars pretty much down so far as delegation of power is concerned, discretionary authority has the broadest possible sweep, and only the uninitiated will leave the agency to its own devices, and take their chances on what the rules will be.

A second consequence of this broad delegation of power to administrative agencies is the overwhelming importance, in the case of the Washington lawyer, of an ability to see and interpret trends, to evaluate directions and speed, and to advise in the light of what is probably best described as an informed hunch.

Certainly it is no longer possible to read the law and render an opinion. Statutory standards are so vague and generalized that only by the gradual evolution of boundaries through agency action do they become meaningful at all. The Securities and Exchange Commission will approve a reorganization under the Public Utility Holding Company Act if it is, among other things, "fair and equitable." The Federal Communications Commission will issue a license to a putative broadcaster if to do so is in "the public convenience, interest or necessity." These provisions are not exceptional in their generality. Even relatively concrete terms are deceptively indefinite – "regular rate of pay" under the Fair Labor Standards Act, for example.

This problem of the Washington lawyer, however,

does not arise solely because of the generality of the basic statutory law. It is further aggravated by the fact that many administrative agencies do not write opinions when they decide cases. Imagine a legal doctrine which has been developed and analyzed at length in judicial opinions, and then imagine the difficulty one would have in advising clients if no more than the decisions themselves were known. Yet recently the Federal Trade Commission has completely reversed a prior position which it had held on the applicability of one section of the Robinson-Patman Act to exporting factors, evidencing its action solely by dismissing one paragraph of a complaint. Many agencies do, of course, write full opinions, but for many more all doctrines, and all of the constant refinement and modification of doctrines, must be painfully unearthed from vast numbers of decisions which recite no more than findings of fact and conclusions of law.

Partly because the customary sources of information are limited, and partly because the essence of administrative action is its kinetic quality, the Washington lawyer must take full advantage of every other source of information. To the extent that "policy" is the guide to agency action, it is up to the lawyer to divine that policy. This is hard to do, and even harder to describe, for the lawyer is dealing with a state of mind — the agency's own view of its objectives. Yet his effectiveness in advising clients depends on a measure of successful guesswork. And so the lawyer turns to the statute, its background and legislative history, to find meaning between lines. He studies the background of the agency's principal personnel, and is aware of the fact that a change in personnel may well modify a policy or a trend. He realizes that the agency's sense of its "mission" is of great significance. He is not surprised to find that when the seniority rights of returning service men came into conflict with union collective bargaining contracts, the Director of Selective Service read the statute as favoring the veteran and the Department of Labor took an opposite view.[8] Indeed, he would be surprised were the positions reversed. Whether such bias is desirable or not, it cannot be ignored.

Frequently more important than the information acquired from any of these sources is what the lawyer can learn from dealings with the agency and its staff. Their comments with respect to the one problem before them frequently have implications for other problems in which the lawyer is interested. Particularly is this true in informal conferences and hearings, for informality encourages candor. For example, the Securities and Exchange Commission has a rule embodying a "no sale theory," whereby certain mergers, consolidations and reclassifications of securities are exempted from the registration provisions of the Securities Act. The rule itself is quite usual in style and tone, but a lawyer who seeks to invoke it will meet surprising resistance. The merger in which his client is interested does not precisely satisfy the letter of the rule, though it is well within the rationale of the "no sale theory."[9] Through discussion with the staff, the lawyer realizes that the Commission has misgivings about the wisdom of its own rule, and may be expected to construe it very strictly. Knowledge of that, at the planning stage of his client's merger or consolidation, may avoid later difficulties.

Sometimes the Washington lawyer is able to identify what we might call the "current thinking" of the agency, which may be translated into future regulations or decisions. The importance which may attach to an agency's "thinking" is illustrated by two recent full-dress law review articles discussing what was frankly described as a "tentatively determined" Treasury policy relating to corporate reorganizations.[10] The full scope and detail of the new Treasury policy were far from clear at the time; the outlines had been gleaned from oral discussions and a number of informal letter rulings, only one of which had ever been published. Yet the tax lawyers who authored the articles properly felt that the prospective development was of great moment to the tax practitioner. The trial balloon is not unknown; an agency will at times deliberately but informally communicate proposed changes in policy to private lawyers, simply to provoke an informative reaction.

The ultimate refinement of this activity occurs when the Washington lawyer can observe a trend toward a new policy which the agency has not yet fully articulated even to itself. The Federal Power Commission has recently announced that in granting certificates for natural gas pipelines, the possession of storage facilities for temporary surplus gas would be a factor to which it would give considerable weight. Actually, long before this consideration was definitely avowed, the Commission had given signs of its concern. A watchful lawyer was in a position to anticipate by advising a client, seeking a certificate for a pipeline, of the desirability of planning storage facilities whenever possible.

The emphasis on the importance of knowing the agency, and on the significance of the decision at the agency level, is underlined by the decreasing importance of the right of judicial review. No more than fifteen or twenty years ago it was not unnatural for the administrative lawyer to regard judicial review as his opportunity for deliverance. Arguments on the constitutional limits of delegation of power were combined with arguments for broad judicial review; the smaller the permissible delegation, and the broader the review, the narrower the agency discretion became, and a case which had been lost might be retrieved. By habit and training, lawyers felt more comfortable in dealing with courts, and there was a sense that they were fulfilling a traditional role in challenging the legality of governmental action before the judiciary.

It has been a losing fight. The cases on delegation of power, which once occupied so prominent a place in briefs on review of administrative action, and so large a share of the casebooks on administrative law, are now of little more than historical interest. On the scope of judicial review, the ammunition provided by the Administrative Procedure Act – particularly the concept in Section 10(e) of review on "the whole record" [11] – has been largely ineffective. The controversy still rages, but unquestionably it is the availability and scope of review which have narrowed, and not administrative discretion. In an area as important as renegotiation, for example, judicial review is very drastically restricted.[12]

Moreover, not only is successful challenge difficult, but even victory may be Pyrrhic. In the famous *Morgan* proceedings, involving the fixing of stockyard rates, the Supreme Court entertained four separate appeals.[13] On the first two appeals, the Court found procedural defects, and indeed the second *Morgan* decision is still a landmark decision in administrative law. On remand, however, the Secretary of Agriculture remedied the defects and fixed the same rates retroactively. In the two later appeals, he was upheld. As a practical matter, respondents were thus back where they started, except for the expenses of judicial review and the very dubious consolation that they had been the vehicles for the making of important administrative law. An interesting sidelight on the process of review is to be found in the fact that the three-judge district court was reversed four times out of four.

Let me make clear, however, that I am not suggesting that judicial review is unimportant. It is important, and it should be available in many more areas than it is now. The very fact of its availability, and the willingness of the Washington lawyer to challenge what he believes to be unfair or illegal, are powerful sanctions toward administrative equity. Overzealous officials will think once, at any rate, even if not twice, before they act. Nor did I mean to imply that it is not frequently invoked. Washington lawyers may even be regarded as overly litigious, either on questions of law, substantive or procedural, or on discretionary decisions which offer any chance for successful challenge. All that I mean to say is that the Washington lawyer has come to realize that his best opportunity to protect his client is at the agency level. He cannot forget about judicial review, but neither can he afford to rely on it.

Let me turn, now, to a second characteristic of administrative agencies. Almost without exception they are alleged to possess expertise. I use "alleged" advisedly, because "expertise" is a word which is heavily overworked. It is more than mere familiarity with a specialized vocabulary behind which an agency takes refuge in deciding basic economic or political issues on which it is by no means uniquely qualified. It is more than a cloak for a predilection or a bias. Yet it is used to describe or justify both of those characteristics, as well as in its true meaning – a unique ability to exercise judgment on some particular question. No doubt some of the difficulty lies with the courts, for it seems to take a judge of some courage to avoid referring to "expertise" in an opinion upholding agency action. A lawyer may well feel that if there is to be judicial abdication, some better reason than "expertise" ought to be found to justify it.

Nevertheless, no Washington lawyer would deny that most agencies operate in areas where expertness is needed, and even that they possess some degree of it, although he might suggest that their actions do not always reflect its exercise. When an agency is first constituted or first charged with a new function, it starts with a series of related and complex problems. Whatever the initial training of its personnel, the very fact of continuously dealing with these problems must leave some residuum of specialized experience. Moreover, many agencies employ and utilize the services of persons who are unquestionably experts – technologists or scientists whose training is relevant to the agency function or the subject matter with which it is concerned.

So far as concerns the administrative agencies themselves, this is scarcely a new or significant conclusion. What may be of interest is the correlative effect on the bar. The Washington lawyer, having to deal with the agency, and therefore with its problems, has increasingly found that he must develop a comparable expertness of his own. It is, indeed, the degree to which expertise is demanded which largely determines the extent to which the Washington lawyer practicing before that particular agency must become a specialist.

In some cases this expertise lies in a working grasp of an immense bulk of complex materials which go to make up the regulatory apparatus. For example, the sheer complexity of the Internal Revenue Code, as supplemented by the even more massive administrative materials, is a major factor in tax specialization. Any lawyer who has sought to thread his way through it will recognize Judge Learned Hand's description of the process:

> . . . In my own case the words of such an act as the Income Tax, for example, merely dance before my eyes in a meaningless procession: cross-reference to cross-reference, exception upon exception — couched in abstract terms that offer no handle to seize hold of — leave in my mind only a confused sense of some vitally important, but successfully concealed, purport, which it is my duty to extract, but which is within my power, if at all, only after the most inordinate expenditure of time.[14]

This statement is not uniquely applicable to the tax statutes, although they are no doubt entitled to the dubious credit of being outstanding in this respect. Our patent and copyright, and our immigration and naturalization laws probably deserve honorable mention, and others are not far behind either in bulk or in esoteric vocabulary. The only course open to the lawyer is to work with the materials until he has acquired familiarity and experience, which is really to say, until he has become a specialist.

There are likewise strong forces impelling specialization where an entire industry is under agency regulation. In those fields, the Washington lawyer is not in a position to make much progress for any client until he has a thorough familiarity, not merely with his client's business, but with the entire industry — its structure, its operating problems, and the like. Moreover, he will have to master, not just one statutory provision and the regulations thereunder, but the whole regulatory scheme.

Let me illustrate: A lawyer for an airline must be concerned not only with the relations between his client and the Civil Aeronautics Board, but he must also watch carefully for agency action in relation to other airlines. A new rate tariff, a request for approval of new services, or of a merger or agreement — all of these may affect our lawyer's hypothetical client, even though proposed by other airlines. They must be examined as they are filed with the Board. But to determine whether his client needs to be concerned, the Washington lawyer must know both his industry facts and his agency law, and keep his knowledge up to date.

In that last simple statement — keeping up to date — lie endless hours of reading. Keeping up to date is no simple task. The agencies themselves supply a persistent stream of material — regulations, rules, orders, decisions and releases. Despite the invaluable digests and summaries of Commerce Clearing House, Prentice-Hall, and the Bureau of National Affairs, this means a daily brief case packed for home consumption. Agency administration is typically dynamic. Frequently, hectic would be a more descriptive word, when either the industry involved is rapidly developing and constantly in flux, as has certainly been true of the airlines and the television and natural gas industries, or when the agency itself is in the development stage, as has been dramatically and painfully true of the present emergency agencies.

Volume and complexity of subject matter are not the only characteristics of a government agency which tend toward specialization among those who practice before it. Agency expertise, particularly but not necessarily in the single-industry regulatory agencies, is also a result of their employment of technical experts of all kinds. Just as in Congress all laws are not written by lawyers, so in administrative agencies all rules and regulations are not proposed, and certainly are not enforced, by members of the legal profession. For example, probably neither the Federal Power Commission nor the Federal Communications Commission could function without the aid of engineers in their respective fields of power and communications. Likewise, it would be a strange Food and Drug Administration without its medical doctors, chemists, toxicologists, nutritionists, bacteriologists, sanitary engineers, and the like.

Here is an expertise which the Washington lawyer must match if he would be effective. To a considerable degree, his answer follows tradition. Long before administrative agencies were important, the lawyer solved the problem of an opposing expert by the simple device of securing the services of an expert of his own. In court proceedings, the effect was often a trial by battle of experts.

In dealing with experts in an agency, the lawyer likewise brings in his own expert. In administrative practice, however, there is one important difference. The role of the expert is as likely to be that of avoiding as of winning an adversary proceeding. An application to the Federal Power Commission for approval of a proposed hydroelectric power project is accompanied by mountains of engineering data. In passing on the application, the Commission will of course consult its engineering staff. Hence, the lawyer's aim is to utilize his client's engineering experts in order to persuade the agency engineers of the merits of his client's proposal, and if possible to avoid battle with anyone.

Apart from this difference, the problem of the Washington lawyer in dealing with the experts on his clients' side of the matter – the scientists, doctors, engineers, accountants, economists, statisticians and all others – is not essentially different from what it has always been. The lawyer and the expert educate each other, the non-lawyer expounding esoteric facts and judgments, the lawyer stressing relevance and procedure. If the lawyer is skillful, each winds up knowing the other's basic approach and what each has to contribute. Lawyers have always felt that "experts [which excludes anyone with a law degree] should remain on tap, not on top." Certainly, I will not undertake to dispute that. Nevertheless, Washington lawyers have discovered that sometimes after the mutual educational process is completed, experts do better alone; informal conferences with agency engineers, for example, are sometimes best conducted by clients' engineers without a lawyer.

Now, let us take up briefly a third aspect of administrative practice, which is very much related to this matter of expertise. The aspect which is disconcerting, rather than laborious, is the extent to which knowledge and experience, painfully acquired, can become almost immediately obsolete.

In the early days of the New Deal, the National Industrial Recovery Act, with its codes for everything, created a whole corps of Washington specialists. Literally overnight, all their knowledge, all their expertise, was perfectly useless. The War Labor Board of World War II is a sample of the same thing: we have a new national effort to control wages, but there are so many points of dissimilarity and so few old faces and old points of view that much of the accumulated wisdom of the 1940's is now irrelevant. I used to consider myself something of an expert on all the ramifications of the "Little Steel Formula." I still remember the formula, but as salable knowledge it is strictly in the antique class. There is somewhat more continuity, as it happens, between the Office of Price Stabilization and the National Production Authority and their World War II counterparts, but in the former, at least, a large share of the difficulty has been that old patterns of control no longer fit a changed economic situation. No doubt the last two decades, particularly the war years, have been unusual, but the Washington lawyer has a short history as a species, and it is hard for him to distinguish norm from aberration. He simply must adjust himself to the occupational hazards.

At this point let me shift to a wholly new frame of reference. Thus far we have considered the activities of the Washington lawyer in the administrative field from the point of view of several characteristics of the agencies with which he deals. Now, let us consider his activities in terms of several types of clients whom he may represent. This, I think, will take us more directly into what the Washington lawyer does. Although lawyers undertake important activities in organized bar committees and groups, as we shall see later, they function primarily and most frequently in relation to concrete problems for specific clients.

It would not be quite realistic to suggest that we take up the administrative process from the client's point of view. We are dealing with the lawyer's work, and he will approach the problem of every client in a lawyer's way. Nevertheless, if we classify clients into three general groups, we can focus on a few aspects of the Washington lawyer's work which relate to each. First, then, there is the client who is not concerned about immediate agency action, but who wants advice as to how he may avoid trouble in the future. Second, there is the client who wishes to pursue a course of conduct which must be passed upon in advance by some agency. Finally, we can consider the client who seeks representation because an agency has taken, or is considering taking, action adverse to his interests.

The Washington lawyer probably is happiest when a client comes to see him before there is a "clear and present danger" of adverse agency action, and while there is still time for lawyer and client between them to practice some preventive law. Many such clients, of course, invoke the lawyer's aid simply to help them keep up with changing rules and new developments. We have seen the trouble the Washington lawyer has in keeping up to date on even the administrative rulings and regulations, and the latest trends, in a *single* agency, but for the usual businessman *many* agencies are important. Representation of any business enterprise involves keeping at least generally familiar with developments in labor relations, wages and hours, taxes, government procurement policies, tariffs, railroad rates — indeed in all of the various aspects of federal administration which impinge, directly or indirectly, on business today. The work is particularly difficult in emergency periods, when complex regulation is proceeding at a dizzying pace. Priorities, allocations, wage and price controls are examples. Here, the lawyer may merely pass along to the client the new rules and regulations, translate them in terms of their particular effect on his situation, and suggest ways and means of obeying them.

Whether the work is of this more or less routine nature, or is counseling on a specific and complicated proposal for action, there seem to me to be two features which are worthy of comment. Perhaps the features are not peculiar to Washington lawyers, because I must admit that my data are scarcely adequate for firm comparison with lawyers who are consulted on problems where the government does not impinge. Government regulation, however, can at least be said to accentuate them.

The first of these two features of the Washington lawyer's counseling function is the extent to which it requires a knowledge of the intimate details of the client's business, an appraisal of business facts, and the making of business judgments. Criticism of this as "client caretaking," and as involving business rather than law, overlooks the nature of government regulations and the sweep of government impact. The lawyer must know the client's method of distribution to advise, for example, on the effect of current doctrine relating to basing points, or quantity discounts, or brokerage payments. He must know his client's principal raw materials and their sources to advise on tariff matters, or agricultural subsidies, or government allocation or stockpile policies. The list could be expanded indefinitely. Activities which have traditionally been purely "business" are becoming "legal" in the sense that they may be crucial to an agency determination. It has been wisely suggested that agency "supervision" is a little-noticed but very important function.[15] It can be added that it becomes the job of the Washington lawyer to anticipate the agency by some advance supervision.

Moreover, the very general and vague standards of legality which have been characteristic of administrative regulation make it almost essential for a client to turn to his lawyer for a judgment which blends business and legal factors. Consider the manufacturer of a branded product who makes payments to retailers who advertise his brand, and is concerned whether his method of computing payments is lawful under the Robinson-Patman Act. His lawyer cannot give him a complete primer of "do's" and "don't's" and tell him to devise a method of making payments which fits the one and avoids the other. The statute is simply too unclear. Indeed, the lawyer may have difficulty deciding whether his client's present practice is lawful or not, for he is working in a vast twilight zone, in which there are all degrees of "maybe." And so, instead of the lawyer's trying to impart to his businessman-client all the subtleties that go to make up legal judgment, he sets out to gather the business facts and to grasp the business objectives, and to devise a method which best mediates the conflicting demands of the business and the law. Do not think that the businessman is overjoyed. The president of a major oil company once described his enterprise as "a small body of businessmen completely surrounded by lawyers." Many a businessman has asked himself, and perhaps even asked his lawyer, whether he might not just as well step out and let the lawyers do it all.

The second aspect of the Washington lawyer's activities as an adviser, and one which I am relatively sure is distinctive, is the extent to which he may, and does, seek governmental advice and guidance. Courts characteristically will not render advisory opinions. Agencies just as characteristically will, even in situations where the law does not compel the client to obtain advance agency clearance, on the theory that it is an aid to effective administration. The result is that even in trying to work out an adjustment of a client's problem, in which the agency has no direct and immediate interest, the lawyer may find himself dealing with the agency.

The lawyer who seeks advance agency guidance, though under no compulsion to do so, may have one of two purposes in mind. First, he may simply want information as to the agency's attitude toward his client's problem. Having analyzed the problem for himself, he will feel more assurance if a knowledgeable staff member concurs in his view. If, on the other hand, the staff member disagrees with him, the lawyer will want to consider the reasons given and to reassess his own analysis. Sometimes the discussion with the staff member will suggest a satisfactory alternative course of action.

Of course, advice of this sort is not always either necessary or desirable. The Washington lawyer may be sufficiently current on agency thinking to know what the answer would be. He is also aware of the danger of drawing the agency's attention to a matter which it might regard unfavorably, even when the conversation with the staff member is on a hypothetical plane. Yet despite these rather special problems, if an agency makes informal advice available, the lawyer will frequently take the opportunity to augment the value of his own aid to his client.

There is one aspect of this which warrants a further comment. The Washington lawyer may wish to get more than the agency's opinion on a problem; he may want to have the agency bind itself, to some degree, to adhere to its position in the future. Whether or not to do so depends, of course, on a number of intangibles: the importance and the doubtfulness of the problem and the relative value of future certainty; the feasibility of giving the facts in such a manner as to cover the transaction, or the course of conduct, for the future; the probability of a favorable ruling and the consequences of an unfavorable one, and the like.

Those are all interesting points, but the aspect on which I think a comment is most warranted is the difficulty which the average lawyer faces in knowing the extent to which any particular agency will give effective advisory opinions. Very few agencies, of course, are willing to bind themselves formally and completely as to future action. In fact, however, most agencies do give some degree of binding effect to their advisory opinions. What degree is obviously a matter of considerable practical importance to the lawyer, yet agency policies in this respect are seldom embodied in rules of procedure. The specialist has an inordinate, and I think largely an unnecessary, advantage.

Historical practice, perhaps trial and error, and the differences in practical situations have led to wide variations from agency to agency. While oral opinions in many agencies have only information value, an agency like the Securities and Exchange Commission will frequently be reluctant to repudiate oral advice given by a staff member with power to do so. The reason makes sense: The Commission feels that it can be more effective if the public learns to accept and rely on the advice of its staff. To the lawyer, however, all of this means he must learn by his own experience, or that of others, just what the practice is of the particular body with which he is dealing. Rarely is it formulated and published.

Similarly, agencies have generally been remiss about publishing the procedural steps which lawyers may or should take in obtaining an advisory opinion. Even the Bureau of Internal Revenue, which has probably developed the advisory function most efficiently and effectively, does not tell the lawyer of considerations he needs to know to utilize Bureau procedure intelligently. The Bureau's rules provide for Treasury closing agreements which will be legally binding, but the experienced tax lawyer knows that such agreements can normally be obtained only after prohibitive delay. They provide for special rulings, which are stated to be not binding, but experience has shown that the Bureau will almost never fail to give these rulings a conclusive weight. They state that rulings will be granted in certain classes of cases, but in fact it is common Bureau practice to issue rulings in other cases. The Regulations do not explicitly provide for conferences in connection with rulings, yet informal conferences are usually granted both before a ruling is requested and while it is pending. The conference prior to request is extremely important, since it gives the lawyer a fair idea of whether his request will be granted. The importance of later conferences lies in the fact that a lawyer can usually withdraw a request, and will often do so if it appears likely to be denied.

I imply no criticism of current Bureau practice. What is important is its failure to articulate, in written form available to all, the procedure actually followed. Even in this respect, the Bureau is better than most. The Federal Register Act and the Administrative Procedure Act represent a step forward, but the information which they evoke seems to date to have been largely limited to formal procedures and formal rules.[16] Of course, there will be situations in which procedure cannot be explained in full detail, or is too unimportant to warrant the effort, but many procedures, like the Bureau example cited above, do not fall in either of those categories. Although the Washington lawyer who specializes before one agency will gain certain inevitable and legitimate advantages, at least knowledge of the agency's procedure should be available to all – specialists and nonspecialists – to the full extent that rules of procedure can be articulated.

Now let us turn to the second type of client — the one who seeks more than guidance, and wants to undertake some course of conduct which requires affirmative approval, or some other affirmative action, by an administrative agency. Again we find so many contexts, and so many variations, that we cannot hope to do more than note one or two principal features.

Let us take a moment, however, to consider the role of the lawyer in one rather distinctive group of cases of this sort — the situation in which he encounters not a regulatory body, but an agency or department that is disbursing benefits of some kind, or is fulfilling the housekeeping needs of the government. What is the role of the lawyer who represents a client who seeks to borrow from the Reconstruction Finance Corporation, the Export-Import or World Bank, or to lease or purchase a plant from the Surplus Property Administrator, or to negotiate a procurement contract with the Department of Defense.

There is here considerable misapprehension, in two directions. Some will assert that the Washington lawyer has no part to play, except as an influence-peddler. If it were as simple as that, it would be easy to resolve at least some of the problems of influence-peddling by prohibiting lawyers from operating in these fields. Actually, it is not; the lawyer does have a role, and influence-peddling is no more than an abusive exercise of a wholly legitimate function.

On the other hand, some will assume that this is an area of peculiarly esoteric activities. Again, to a considerable extent, they will be wrong. In large part, the lawyer's function here is no different from what it would be were his client dealing with a private party. An application for a sizable loan from the Reconstruction Finance Corporation raises the same problems as would an application to the First National Bank of any city. The lawyer will marshal all of the relevant data to show his client's need for the loan and his qualifications to receive it, and he will then organize the data with maximum persuasive effect. In the negotiations and preparation of the necessary papers, he will again perform traditional functions of draftsmanship, interpretation, and the visualization of problems that may arise in the performance of the particular agreement.

There is an area of special competence, of course, for the fact that the government is a party to the transaction will require special adjustments. The Export-Import Bank is not the First National Bank; it has a statutory policy to implement, and the lawyer must understand that policy, including the political factors that may come into play. If the client is seeking a government contract, the lawyer will be called upon to consider a diverse assortment of problems. Can the client negotiate or must he proceed by bids? What is likely to be the impact of, say, the Walsh-Healey Act on the client? How is he affected by provisions for termination, or tentative price-fixing, which are so common in current government contracts? All of these are certainly important, and fully warrant experienced legal guidance.

This field of activity, in common with practically all fields in which the Washington lawyer is attempting to make the government take action, is characterized by the use of informal procedures. They have such general utility, and at the same time involve such real dangers, that they warrant examination.

Informal procedures are not, of course, confined

to situations where formal procedures are unavailable. When a client files a registration statement for approval by the Securities and Exchange Commission, formal procedures are available for testing its adequacy. The Commission, however, is not primarily interested in defeating the client's aims, but rather in seeing that certain standards are complied with. It has power to disapprove the registration statement on the proposed issue, thereby instituting an adversary stop-order proceeding. But the Commission's job is even more effectively done if the registration statement is adequate when it is filed. The Commission, therefore, seeks to give prospective registrants all the help toward compliance that it can. The experienced securities lawyer is encouraged to check with the Commission staff on doubtful problems before he finishes the preparation of the statement, and to check again just before filing, in order to gain maximum possible assurance that it will not be disapproved. Even after the statement is filed, if there develops opposition to some feature of the statement, the lawyer will seek through informal negotiations to find a basis of agreement. Although a stop-order proceeding affords a full hearing and judicial review, its initiation will usually frustrate the securities issue.

Moreover, the informal process has outstanding advantages in efficiency of time and effort and in flexibility which enables rapid identification of the crucial issues, so that arguments may be directed to them, until agreement is reached or it becomes clear that it cannot be voluntarily obtained.

Let me illustrate with a proceeding before the State Department's Passport Division. The client has already been refused a passport on the ground that he has been expatriated and is no longer a citizen. At this point, the lawyer is retained. A judicial proceeding *de novo* is available on this issue, but his client needs the passport without delay and the lawyer seeks reconsideration, files a memorandum setting forth his client's position, and is granted a conference with an official of the Division. He sets forth four separate arguments as to why there has been no expatriation, but he stresses one in particular because he thinks that is his best. Somewhat to his surprise, the official indicates interest in one of the other arguments, and suggests that if the necessary facts to support it can be shown, he might recommend a reversal of the Division's stand.

The conference over, the lawyer hastens to gather the evidence needed to comply. He submits it, and shortly thereafter a passport issues.

Had the proceeding been a formal adversary hearing from the outset, the lawyer would have had no notion of what issues the agency thought crucial. He would have had to guess at what to include in his case and what to exclude, and where to put his main emphasis. He might have guessed wrong; indeed, in the instance I have described, he probably would have. A court might ultimately have vindicated his client, but the delay would have been ruinous. This is a familiar problem to the courtroom advocate, but it is considerably alleviated by the informal conference method which administrative agencies can utilize.

For many agencies, of course, the necessities of speed and flexibility make any sort of hearing procedure impossible. The Wage Stabilization Board obviously could not function if it were necessary to have a hearing on every proposal for a wage increase, or the National Production Authority on every request for critical material. The Reconstruction Finance Corporation quite properly processes applications for loans on the papers submitted, and does not set the matter down for hearing.

Yet informal procedures raise problems, both in the agencies where they supplement the formal procedures, and in the agencies where no formal procedures are provided. Inevitably, they broaden still more the scope of agency discretion, and such discretion may be readily abused. If there is no check on agency discretion, such as the very real brake provided by the requirement of a hearing, the agency may not only assume authority which Congress has not sanctioned, but may also utilize its discretion to give preferences to certain persons that cannot be justified on the merits. And I do not refer only to undue influence and favoritism; improper preference may just as easily be due to incompetence.

The possibility of abuse, however, even when experience has shown it to be real and not speculative, should not lead us blindly to discard informal procedures and to put agency personnel into a strait-jacket. True, we might insure that nothing that was done would be improper, but the incidental effect might be that nothing was done at all. Aside from the obvious and overriding need for topflight personnel to exercise discretionary power, there are few easy generalizations. Certainly, agencies should make every effort to articulate the legal standards which they apply, but the extent to which this can be done will vary from agency to agency and even from case to case. The importance of their publishing their procedures we have already discussed. The aim – perhaps not entirely attainable – should be to convince the businessman that he does not need to retain a lawyer merely to find out which official in what agency handles a certain matter. Studies might throw light on the usefulness of certain safeguards against improper or incorrect agency action, such as enforced publicity, intra-agency review practices, and the relatively new congressional "watchdog" committees. Concentration on how we can best improve the functioning of the informal processes, rather than condemnation, is obviously the best approach.

Informal procedures also bring to the fore certain ethical problems for the Washington lawyer. We have already discussed Canon 26 of the Canons of Professional Ethics in terms of non-public legislative activities. The Canon applies equally to "advocacy of claims before departments of government." The same ambiguities and difficulties inherent in the phrase "secret personal solicitation" also bedevil one who seeks an ethical evaluation of the activities of Washington lawyers in informal, non-public, agency proceedings. What was said before is equally applicable here – the Canon is so all-inclusive in scope and so vague in standard as to be largely unworkable.

Yet this much can be said. Where there is a formal administrative hearing, any informal, off-the-record contacts with the person who will make the decision should certainly be held to a minimum. Section 5(c) of the Administrative Procedure Act, which seeks to insulate, within each agency, the investigating and prosecuting personnel from those who are responsible for agency adjudication, is aimed at this objective, though it provides exemptions. The Civil Aeronautics Board has taken a still further step. Its principles of practice include the provision that in cases to be decided after hearing and on a record:

> It is improper that there be any private communication on the merits of the case to a member of the Board

or its staff or to the examiner in the case by any person, either in private or public life, unless provided by law.[17]

The objective, of course, must be to preserve the integrity of the quasi-judicial process, and at the same time not to endanger the viability of the administrative process as a whole. Everything I have said indicates the danger of generalization, and certainly I am not prepared to say that the Civil Aeronautics Board rule would work equally well in other agencies. The tripartite boards like the Wage Stabilization Boards raise questions all their own. On this problem, too, much more work is still to be done.

There remain for consideration those clients who, frequently in an unhappy frame of mind, come to the Washington lawyer because some agency is taking action, or may take action, which will unfavorably affect them. Such action may take several forms. It may be directed specifically against the client, as by a charge that he has violated one of the myriad of laws which surrounds him, or perhaps that he has merely earned too much money under a contract directly or indirectly performed for the government, and must pay some back by renegotiation. Or the agency may be considering a request for approval made by some other private person, which if granted would be adverse to the client. Still another possibility is that the agency is considering the issuance or amendment of a regulation which will be general in purport and effect, but may have a very particularized impact on the client.

From the lawyer's point of view, the problems of defending a client against governmental prosecution are in their broadest form not unlike those we have been discussing. The usual progression is from informal proceedings to a formal hearing. The case starts with an agency investigation leading to a decision on the filing of a complaint; it may progress to informal negotiations for settlement prior to hearing; finally, it may reach formal hearing and decision. Cases involving prosecution, however, have an important and pervasive difference in atmosphere. From the outset, the proceeding has an adversary flavor which it never loses.

Most lawyers, I believe, would say that the formal hearing plays a more important role in truly adversary cases than in other types of agency proceedings, but I suspect that the generalization is at least questionable. It is true that a full hearing is always available at some stage of the proceeding. In practice, however, there are times when it is not worth much. Thus, multiple seizures of some types of misbranded articles may be made upon an agency determination reached without a hearing or judicial review.[18] The hearing which follows seizure will almost certainly be insufficient to repair the damage done, and the only useful recourse of lawyer and client is to informal negotiations before seizure. Taking a somewhat different example, a railroad may be reluctant to carry to formal hearing an Interstate Commerce Commission charge that its service violates some rule. If the point at issue is minor, when compared to the railroad's obvious interest in not antagonizing the Commission, the railroad may well agree to a change in service worked out informally and without a contest. And even when a hearing is available in practice as well as in legal theory, the lawyer will nevertheless want to canvass his client's situation for possibility of settlement.

The investigative stage of a hearing usually offers the best opportunity for termination of the proceeding without all-out battle. The agency attitude may range from the completely open-minded curiosity of a revenue agent making a routine field audit, to the suspicions of a Regional Director of the National Labor Relations Board who has received a detailed and documented charge accusing the client of unfair labor practices. In any event, the agency's own view of the facts and the law may not yet have jelled, and to a greater or lesser degree, its staff is open to counterargument. The lawyer will want to be kept informed by the client on the data the investigators are examining and he will seek to discern the legal theory on which they are proceeding. And he will overlook no opportunity to bring to the agency's attention his client's view of the facts it is eliciting and his own legal theories as to their significance. Usually there is much to be gained and little to be lost in adopting an attitude of cooperation toward investigators in their work.

If investigation convinces the agency that it has a case requiring further action, it will file a complaint which creates a formal adversary relationship. Negotiation, however, remains available and is frequently successful. Broadly speaking, the situation is not unlike that between adversaries in a case awaiting trial in court, and I shall not attempt to delve into the many forms which negotiations may take. Of passing interest is the diversity of viewpoints which different agencies take toward negotiated settlements. At one extreme is the Renegotiation Board, which seems to feel that it can operate most effectively by doing what its name implies – negotiating almost all of its cases. Somewhere near the other end of the spectrum, at least until recently, was the Federal Trade Commission, which prior to 1951 would not permit any settlement after a complaint issued, except upon a formal admission of facts essential to show a violation. Its reversal of this position was reached only after long and continuous urging, both by private practitioners and by others.

The problem of the client who wants to participate in a proceeding initiated by some third person's request for agency approval need not detain us. The very fact that the client is unfavorably affected gives the proceeding an adversary character, and the lawyer's activities fall into the framework we have been discussing, except that the problem is one of reconciling or deciding between the conflicting interests of private parties.

Agency rule-making, on the other hand, brings

the lawyer into an administrative arena quite different from those we have been considering, and perhaps more closely akin to the lawyer's activities before the legislature. Rule-making is as unlimited in the scope of its subject matter as Congress and the agency choose to make it. Consider, for example, the recent proceeding before the Federal Communications Commission, as a result of which the Commission promulgated allocations of some two thousand television frequencies to cities over the entire length and breadth of the United States. The complexities of the undertaking were enormous. Engineering decisions had to be made as to the distances that must exist between stations having the same or adjacent channels. Judgments on considerations such as economic and population data were necessary to determine which city would be granted how many stations. It is almost impossible to give a more concrete description than "public interest" to the factors that determined when to set aside channels solely for educational use. The procedural arrangements for literally hundreds of interested parties demanded a nice balance between the desirability of a full hearing for everyone and the danger of a breakdown of the entire proceeding.

Yet a client who is interested in building and operating a television station in a particular city is just as effectively precluded by a rule-making determination to allocate no additional channels to that city as by any later adjudicatory determination that some other person, not this client, shall be granted a license.

Here we have a vital feature of rule-making. While the problems considered and decisions reached by the agency are of general purport, they will inevitably have a particularized impact on the lawyer's client. How helpful the lawyer can be to his client and to the agency varies from case to case. The lawyer may perform a vital role merely by presenting the agency with facts. That the agency has conducted its own investigation does not necessarily mean that it is up to date, or that it has all the data, or that its statistical summaries correspond to working realities. It is the Washington lawyer who will frequently see the particular impact of a proposed regulation long before the agency sees it – simply because a client's concrete problem causes him to focus first on the particular problem. To illustrate by a somewhat unusual type of "fact," a company recently found that it was subject to a court antitrust decree ordering it to readjust certain differentials in its price structure and also to price regulations freezing all of its prices as they had been. One order could not be obeyed without violating the other. Here, an explanation of the problem to the Office of Price Stabilization brought a modified regulation permitting obedience to the decree.

Again, the lawyer's contribution may well be measured, in large part, by the particular rule-making procedure which is adopted. He has an obvious role, similar to the one we have already mentioned, when rule-making follows the basic pattern of notice of a proposed rule in the Federal Register, with written submissions required to be filed by a certain date. Sometimes written responses to earlier comments are permitted, and sometimes the whole procedure is followed by an open hearing. The lawyer has a similar role in the rather unusual procedure utilized by the Food and Drug Administration in the promulgation of food standards which is preceded by a hearing just as formal as the usual adjudicatory proceeding before an agency, with both oral testimony and full right of cross-examination permitted. On the other hand, the lawyer's role will be substantially different in those agencies which have devised the technique of obtaining the views of interested parties at private and informal conferences. The Board of Governors of the Federal Reserve System, to use a notable example, finds this procedure necessary in promulgating such rules as those relating to rediscount rates, where advance secrecy is essential. Certainly it could not be widely adopted, but for the Board of Governors it has worked out well in practice because of the limited and well-defined group of persons to be consulted.

Rule-making, in other words, shares in the diversity of practice which is characteristic of the administrative process. At the beginning of this chapter, I noted the existence of great variety in administrative procedures, and I have repeated it many times in touching on specific problems. Viewed in the abstract, perhaps it amounts to no more than boring repetition, but it seems to me that it poses an important problem for all who are interested in the future of the administrative process. For, after all, fair and effective procedure lies at the heart of that process. And there is work still to be done to improve administrative procedure.

A great deal has already been done. The Administrative Procedure Act represents a clear forward movement. This is not the time to endorse or criticize its details, or to resolve its ambiguities. Its importance lies in the fact that it represents an effort to set minimum standards of proper agency procedure. That is a worth-while effort, which will undoubtedly be carried forward in the interpretation and perhaps the amendment of that Act.

General minimum standards, however, are not enough. The problem is not merely to find the lowest common denominator which can be applied to all agencies. It is also to try to determine what procedure is best in a particular agency in dealing with a particular kind of problem. What is best for one agency is not even workable for another. To cite an extreme example, the extraordinary impact of national security considerations on the Atomic Energy Commission has led to the adoption of radically different rules of procedure in matters before it. That procedures will and should vary, however, does not mean that the task is hopeless.

The aim must be to attain the best procedure, rather than merely to avoid the worst. That can be done only by the laborious and painstaking approach of considering one agency at a time, and even one problem at a time within an agency. In this task, neither Congress nor the Courts are likely to offer the solution. A legislature which has had to delegate broad substantive powers because it cannot cope with the complexity and detail which their exercise entails, is not likely to delve into the many details of procedure. And the courts have rather vigorously limited their review of agency procedure to seeing that minimum standards are observed.

The job, in other words, is one for the agencies themselves. Unfortunately, when an agency is young and growing, its substantive program necessarily comes first, and procedure frequently gets only incidental consideration. Then, when the agency reaches maturity, the very procedures which have been devised hurriedly and without thorough deliberation are so ingrained through usage that they are hard to change.

Nevertheless, if the agencies are willing to cooperate, much can be done, both by the Washington lawyers and by the law schools. We shall see in the next chapter something of what has already been done. The lawyer, after all, is the one who knows how the rules operate and often, from painful experience, how they fail to operate. Particularly if he is a specialist in the practice before a particular agency, he will be able to combine his practical experience with a realistic appreciation of the problems on the agency side as well. In cooperation with the law schools, which can contribute the time, the continuity, and the scholarship which the practicing lawyer usually does not have, he can do much to improve the formal rules, increase the utility and availability of informal procedures, and clarify the ethical problems. Such work would be very much worth while.

III. Some Reflections on the Role of the Washington Lawyer

IN APPROACHING the conclusion of our discussion, it is appropriate to recall where we began. We noted the relatively recent and increasingly accentuated trend toward economic interdependence and integration. Paralleling that, government itself has been undergoing a gradual, but drastic, revolution in its size, its attitudes, its complexities, and its impact on the national life.

The concurrent effect of these changes on the bar as a whole was admirably summed up by the late Chief Justice Stone some eighteen years ago in an address entitled "The Public Influence of the Bar." [1] What he said has been challenged by some, resented by others, but nonetheless has posed problems that cannot be ignored:

> . . . No longer does [the lawyer's] list of clients represent a cross section of society; no longer do his contacts make him the typical representative and interpreter of his community. The demands of practice are more continuous and exacting. He has less time for reflection upon other than immediate professional undertakings. He is more the man of action, less the philosopher and less the student of history, economics, and government. . . .
>
> The rise of big business has produced an inevitable specialization of the Bar. The successful lawyer of our day more often than not is the proprietor or general manager of a new type of factory, whose legal product is increasingly the result of mass production methods. . . . More and more he must look for his rewards to the material satisfactions derived from profits as from a successfully conducted business, rather than to the intangible and indubitably more durable satisfactions which are to be found in a professional service more consciously directed toward the advancement of the public interest.[2]

We have already seen that for the Washington lawyer, the trends noted by Chief Justice Stone are sharply accentuated. He has been called into being, as it were, by the emergence of big government. He has specialized and adapted his skills to meet the problems which that government creates for the complex that is business and industry. By the very process of adjusting the intimate details of a business organization to the mandates of government regulation he necessarily is injected into the day-to-day operations of his clients. In short, the Washington lawyer has had to cope with "demands of practice [which] are more continuous and exacting," and with the "inevitable specialization of the Bar."

The question which naturally suggests itself is – to what extent are the comments of Chief Justice Stone, made eighteen years ago, applicable to the present-day Washington lawyer? That is a broad question – a very broad question. I cannot expect to do more than give you what the title of this chapter indicates – a few reflections. Perhaps I may hope to inspire further efforts and further thinking on the part of others.

Any assessment of the "public influence of the bar" as applied to the Washington lawyer must start with the recognition that he functions in two distinct frameworks. First, and most often, he is engaged in representing clients in their dealings with the government. Second, he may participate, independently of any client, in action by an organized group, through a bar association or otherwise, to modify, strengthen or improve some particular aspect of governmental or community activity. Let us look at each in turn, considering what function the lawyer can serve, and some of the problems of fulfillment.

It is perhaps strange-sounding, but nonetheless profoundly true doctrine, that the Washington lawyer, in the very process of representing clients, has important influence on government. The influence – perhaps "effect" would be a word less subject to the overtones which I will come to later – is to a considerable degree haphazard, sporadic, even almost accidental. What the Washington lawyer does, and how he does it, both depend on the problems of the clients whose interests he seeks to protect, in *their* relations with the federal government. The measure of these problems is in a sense the measure of his contribution. Nevertheless, it is fair to say that he is an essential participant if the governmental process, as we now know it, is to function effectively.

The effect on government which comes from the work of representing clients is perhaps at the same time most significant and least understood in the area where there is little contact with the government itself. That is the function which the lawyer performs in simply advising his clients, but in which he is in fact operating as an extension of the government's enforcement machinery.

It falls to the lawyer to interpret the statutory mandate in the sense of making clear, or at least clearer, what is meant by long and complex sentences, elaborate cross-references, involved subparagraphs and sub-subparagraphs, and all of the other devices which seem to be the inevitable fruit of any legal commandment. The word "gobbledygook" does not come into our vocabulary without reason.

That is all important and necessary, but even an understandable "thou shalt not" is sterile unless it has a reason, a "why." One cannot hope to conduct his affairs in accordance with the law unless he has a sense of the general pattern into which the particular rules are woven, and can also get a sense of the general wrongness or rightness of what he plans to do. What I have in mind is only the generalized manifestation of the felt need which motivates the preliminary "findings and declaration of policy" which occur in many statutes. In the administrative field, a noteworthy example is the form of ceiling price regulations of the Office of Price Stabilization; each regulation is accompanied by a "Statement of Considerations" and an introductory section entitled "What This Regulation Does," both setting out in simple English the regulation's general scope and purpose.

There is likewise a direct reflection of this constant emphasis on the "why" of the law in the extent to which lawyers study the legislative history of statutes, the annual reports of administrative agencies, and the speeches of administrators and policy makers. Indeed, the lawyers' devotion to legislative histories has prompted the comment that the text of a statute is never referred to unless the legislative history is not clear. Whether it has become too important – whether the real law is now written in the statute books or buried in the relative inaccessibility of legislative history materials – has recently been vigorously questioned by Mr. Justice Jackson.[3] To the extent that the criticism is warranted, the Washington lawyer, in Washington, at least, has an enormous advantage.

This is, of course, traditional legal work so far as statutes are concerned. There is a difference, however, between explaining, in the sense both of interpreting and of rationalizing, an Act of Congress, and in explaining, in the same sense, a regulation of the Wage Stabilization Board dealing with, let us say, year-end bonuses. That cannot be done from books, no matter how extensive one's library facilities may be. Fundamentally, as we saw in Chapter II, it calls for a combination of general expertise and an access to unwritten sources of information — conferences with the industry and labor people, the lawyers, the enforcement staff and others at the Board, all of whom together can supply the information necessary to understand the thinking behind the regulation and its accompanying formal explanation. Nor are the current defense agencies exceptional; they simply present an aggravated and concentrated dose of controls whose counterparts can be found in only slightly less volume and importance in non-emergency periods. The constant rulings and modifications of rulings in the Bureau of Internal Revenue are cases in point.

This work of the Washington lawyer in making the mandates of government meaningful is both a part of the lawyer's professional responsibility and a long step toward enforcement. As a Washington tax lawyer has said, "the Government is entitled to the tax lawyer's help in explaining to taxpayers the necessity and reasonableness of many provisions which taxpayers must inevitably dislike."[4] Without this assistance which the lawyer can give – advice to the client on what the government expects him to do and not to do – the government simply could not operate. Perhaps, if laws and rules and regulations were not written in the expectation that the lawyers would perform this function, there would be simple laws and rules and regulations which laymen could understand – but it would be a very much less intensive and a very different government than we now have.

But explanations and interpretations are not the whole of the Washington lawyer's contribution to the enforcement of the law. He is consulted by his clients on a proposed course of action, a proposed contract, a proposed form of advertising, a proposed almost everything. He says no, and the proposal is abandoned or modified. To me that is just as significant as an injunction obtained by the government against the same proposal. For every occasion on which the government itself prevents some unlawful course of dealing, either *in limine,* or after it has begun, there must be dozens which have been prevented by the refusal of a lawyer to approve them.

This is not to say that the Washington lawyer always can say yes or no. We have already made this point, but it will bear repetition. The antitrust laws, for example, are enacted by Congress in general terms, and their particular area of application is marked out in an endless series of administrative orders and judicial opinions and decrees. What is an "unreasonable restraint of trade" depends on what, probably years later, a court of last resort concludes from all the particular circumstances. No one can give a really meaningful definition of "competition" or "monopoly," or of what constitutes conduct which may "tend . . . to injure, destroy or prevent competition" within the meaning of Section 2(a) of the Robinson-Patman Act. Examples could be multiplied ad infinitum. There are situations in which it appears to be inevitable that in complying with the Robinson-Patman Act the client will necessarily violate the Sherman Act, and vice versa. Clients, and lawyers, necessarily balance legal risks against business risks. Yet despite all of that, I am convinced that my generalization holds: private lawyers, such as the Washington lawyers who specialize in the antitrust field, do more toward enforcing the antitrust laws than ten times as big a government could ever do.

Here you may suspect I am naïve, but I am confident I am not guilty. Most clients, whether they be businessmen, labor unions, or just ordinary citizens, do not employ Washington lawyers to tell them how they can violate the federal laws and get away with it. Most clients do not ask for advice on a particular course of action, and then, upon learning that it cannot legally be followed, proceed with it anyway. Most clients seek assistance in helping them obey the laws as they are.

True, they may, and do, get them changed. There the Washington lawyer has a function in connection with the legislative and quasi-legislative processes, which we have already discussed. And let me add that I do not seek to create the impression that the American public is motivated by the philosophy that "virtue is its own reward." The consequences of being caught – involving not only civil and criminal penalties but the possibility of private actions such as treble damage suits, and the "public relations" aspects of the attendant publicity – are an ever present consideration. But my point does not depend on motives. Whatever the reasons why clients come to lawyers, they do come, and in serving them the lawyers serve the government as well.

But the effects on the government which result

from the practice of the Washington lawyer do not stop here. They go much deeper than the lawyer's functions in interpreting and rationalizing the government's problems to the client, and helping to enforce the government's mandates. In serving his client, the Washington lawyer also performs what is in a sense the converse of that — the interpreting of the client's problems to the government. Particularly is this true in his practice before the executive and administrative agencies.

This is not the occasion to explore the basic philosophy of the lawyer's function, and to apply that philosophy to practice in government cases. Let me merely generalize by asserting, without exploring, the thesis that what the lawyer seeks for his client is a fair deal, in the sense of equal treatment before the law and before the various governmental agencies which administer the law. To achieve that, he will bring to bear all the skill and ability that he has. Let me put to one side, as not truly important in the over-all picture, the lawyers who seek preferential treatment, legally or otherwise. Certainly they exist and government must recognize that they do, but the lawyer's role is not built on that basis.

In the traditional legal proceeding, a trial, this function of the lawyer in getting fair and equal treatment for his client is in two parts. He presents and urges his version of the facts, and he presents and urges his views on the law. Where the law is developing, he urges his view of what it should be.

Before an administrative agency, his function is only superficially different. Indeed, before a quasi-judicial body it is not different at all. The impact he has on the development of the law may be greater than in a judicial proceeding, because the usual quasi-judicial agency is not quite so wedded to *stare decisis*. Moreover, every agency, before it accumulates a full body of precedents, is in a position not unlike that of the Supreme Court in the early nineteenth century, when the Court's case-by-case development of the law was profoundly influenced by the arguments and briefs of eminent counsel. It would not do to overestimate, but it is equally wrong to underestimate, the similar role of lawyers in developing the new concepts of unfair competition, public convenience and necessity, bargaining in good faith, and all the other phrases which gradually have been taking meaningful form as one case has succeeded another.

This is plainly true, as I have said, in the quasi-judicial agencies, but it is equally true, even if less obviously so, in the administrative areas where the dealings with the government are not adversary in form. Here, it is fair to say, the function of the lawyer as the master of the facts relating to his client is more important. When a lawyer assists in an application for a loan from the Reconstruction Finance Corporation, or an export permit, or a certificate of accelerated amortization, or approval of a pension plan, his principal role is to marshal completely, accurately, and effectively, the facts upon which the application is based. The significance of all this is that the government is not automotive; it does not operate until these facts are brought to it for it to evaluate. The Reconstruction Finance Corporation does not go searching for people to make loans to, nor does the Department of Commerce seek out exporters to license. The lawyer who plays a part in getting the facts before the government in a form ripe for decision is almost a *sine qua non* of its effective operation.

There are undoubtedly proceedings of this kind in which there are no legal questions at all. In the usual case, however, there are questions of powers, of limitations, of procedures, of interpretations and applications, of public policy and of all sorts of combinations of them. Again, in the case-by-case development which is hammered out by the arguments of the government lawyer on the one hand and the private lawyer on the other, the Washington lawyer wields a potent influence. Indeed, it may be greater than it is in the courts or in quasi-judicial proceedings, for the range of potential development in such a matter as renegotiation, for example, where only the most general principles were originally decreed, is very wide.

In many areas the impact may be even more substantial because it occurs in a more fundamental way. An agency issues tentative rules or regulations and sets them down for public hearing. The influence of the Washington lawyer who participates in that hearing is substantial, not only in presenting the facts upon which intelligent agency action must be predicated, but in urging the considerations of public policy and of law which he believes should be accepted. To put it another way, in administrative lawmaking, the lawyer is far more important than in legislative lawmaking.

These are, of course, only examples of the work of

the Washington lawyer which we covered in more detail earlier, and it would serve no purpose now to multiply them. In a sense, it is all obvious. My reason for dwelling upon it at this length is only that it is generally not considered from the point of view that we are discussing here. The government is too often regarded, particularly by laymen, as a vast, insensitive mass, shaped by some mysterious inner force of its own. It is far from that, and although it is by no means putty, it does depend on, and its shape and direction and pace are profoundly determined by, the arguments of counsel on the law and by the impact of the facts which they muster and present.

When we reach that conclusion, however – the conclusion that the Washington lawyer has a part to play in the processes of the federal government – we cannot avoid the next step. We must deal with the challenge which Chief Justice Stone put to the entire bar. To what extent, in other words, are the professional services of the Washington lawyer "directed toward the public interest"?

Probably no one would assert that Washington lawyers – or lawyers generally, for that matter – are as aware of the public interest as they should be.

Three years ago, in defending the bar against criticism of its conservatism and its unawareness of the public concern with its activities, Robert T. Swaine admitted:

> . . . Probably too frequently our advice has been too limited to the technical validity of proposed action without regard to its social or economic implications . . .[5]

Nonetheless, only one far more confident and far wiser than I would venture to say just where, and to what degree, the lawyer should temper the fundamental tenet of the profession – loyalty to the client – by economic, social and political considerations.

Yet there are some things that can be said. Let us state one aspect of the problem in terms of the Washington lawyer's legislative activity, for in that area it was posed many years ago by Mr. Justice Brandeis.[6] He stated the problem in terms of activities intended to affect legislative action – what we have called lobbying. After describing the situation in a judicial proceeding, where single-minded, vigorous advocacy is balanced by an adversary equally single-minded and vigorous, the Justice continues:

> But when lawyers act upon the same principle in supporting the attempts of their private clients to secure or to oppose legislation, a very different condition is presented. In the first place, the counsel selected to represent important private interests possesses usually ability of a high order, while the public is often inadequately represented or wholly unrepresented. That presents a condition of great unfairness to the public. As a result many bills pass in our legislatures which would not have become law if the public interest had been fairly represented; and many good bills are defeated which if supported by able lawyers would have been enacted. Lawyers have, as a rule, failed to consider this distinction between practice in the court involving only private interests and practice before the legislature or city council where public interests are involved. Some men of high professional standing have even endeavored to justify their course in advocating professionally legislation which in their character as citizens they would have voted against . . .[7]

In 1905, when that was written, Congress had not delegated widely to administrative agencies. Had the Justice written a half-century later, he would no doubt have included in his comment not only the legislature and the city council, but also the board, the bureau, and the agency. Except for the truly quasi-judicial agencies, most of the executive and administrative agencies and departments are equally subject, with the legislative branch, to what might be called ex parte approaches.

I recognize, as you will have, that the Justice has here brought in an additional problem – the possibility of injustice from loading all the legal competence on one side of a controversy. Put that aside for a moment, however, and look at the problem as the Justice poses it – the lawyer advocating professionally in a non-adversary proceeding, a position which, as a private citizen, he would oppose.

Were we to decree by canon that such conduct was unethical, we would certainly take a long step toward relieving the alleged congestion of the bar. Lawyers who represent clients in dealings with the government cannot be assumed to certify that the public interest is always best served by what they seek for their clients. If that appears to be too great a concession, consider the following:

In some areas where the Washington lawyer operates, neither the lawyer nor the client can possibly know enough to have an opinion on where the public interest lies. We now have controls over the use of scarce materials, the exact allocations being determined by facts relating to a wide variety of industrial uses and business situations, and by evaluation of such imponderables as the policy of containment of Communist aggression and the sociological consequences of scattered local unemployment. A brewery wants more tin plate allocated to beer cans, and retains a Washington lawyer to present its arguments to the officials in Washington who make the basic allocation. No one, I believe, would say that the lawyer, before he can properly accept the retainer, must satisfy himself that beer is more important than beans, or that glass bottles would not do equally well under all the circumstances. The government official, supplied with the facts upon which the lawyer makes his case for beer, but equally in possession of other materials which all the resources of government bring him for his guidance, assumes the responsibility for, and must make the decision on, the public interest.

Consider also the fact that in many areas what may seem to be ex parte proceedings are considerably tinged with adversary characteristics. My tinplate allocator is analogous to a judge, and as to him it is perhaps proper to regard my brewery lawyer as proceeding ex parte. But contrast a situation where a client retains a Washington lawyer to attempt to persuade the Wage-Hour Administrator that the

Fair Labor Standards Act does not apply to a particular industry, or to a particular course of conduct because it is intrastate. Or consider the tax lawyer who is urging a position for his client upon the attorneys in the Bureau of Internal Revenue. Neither the Administrator nor the Bureau attorneys are judges; they are enforcement officers, and can properly be approached by the Washington counsel as an adversary party. Judge Learned Hand has stated it well:

> . . . [The] position of a public officer, charged with the enforcement of a law is different from one who must decide a dispute. If there is a fair doubt, his duty is to present the case for the side which he represents, and leave decision to the court, or the administrative tribunal, upon which lies the responsibility of decision. If he surrenders a plausible construction, it will, at least it may, be surrendered forever; and yet it may be right. . . . [Such] rulings need not have the detachment of a judicial, or semi-judicial decision, and may properly carry a bias . . .[8]

Consider, too, the number of times when the lawyer is faced with a situation in which the goal — "the public interest" — is itself in issue. There certainly is no basis for a conclusive presumption that the government agency is always acting in the public interest. The very case which evoked the statement by Judge Hand which I have just quoted is a not infrequent illustration — two agencies of the government taking precisely opposite sides in the same controversy. Perhaps the issue is, in fact, no more than which part of the public is to be protected, as in the recent butter-margarine controversy. Fair trade acts, not long ago again in the arena of public debate because of the Supreme Court's decision in the *Schwegmann* case,[9] present the problem of whether the consumer or the distributor requires more protection. Again, the need for revenue, certainly a public interest, conflicts with the public interest in agricultural cooperatives. The public interest in a domestic hemp supply, which would free us from reliance upon imports of a vital commodity, is met with the fact that the leaves of the plant provide a rich source of narcotics such as hashish. The debate over the "meeting competition" concept of the Robinson-Patman Act, as it is currently posed, is a debate on whether to protect competitors or to protect competition.

One of the reasons we have political parties, and disagreements within those parties, is that there is no agreement on where the public interest lies.

Moreover, the present-day lawyer in Washington is often faced with a situation in which the goal – the "public interest" – is curiously vague and indeterminate. Just why does – or did – the Reconstruction Finance Corporation lend money to the snake farm and decorative cactus growers? We welter under a hodge-podge of confusing, conflicting, and ever changing ideas of what best serves the country.

But even though all this can be said, it is nevertheless not a complete answer. What Justice Brandeis had in mind was not a canon of ethics, but a personal standard by which we judge not only the clients we are willing to represent, but also the extent to which we will seek to include in our professional advice and assistance a consideration of national affairs. We have an obligation to do more than tell clients how they can lawfully do what they want to do. I do not refer only to the clients who want to urge positions so outrageous that no lawyer could advocate them and still maintain his self-respect. We should go beyond that. The public position of the bar suffers, and properly so, when it becomes apparent that there are Washington lawyers who are quite willing to ignore entirely the larger interests of the country and the basic standards of decency in the process of stringing together sets of legal loopholes to achieve some inordinate advantage. Because this is an area in which canons of ethics and Grievance Committees cannot operate is the more reason why all lawyers should be alert to the implicit, as well as the explicit, responsibilities which distinguish law as a profession, not merely a highly technical trade.

Now let us turn to the other aspect of Justice Brandeis's problem – the danger of weighting the scales against the public interest by concentrating all the legal ability on one side. That problem, on the surface, would appear to relate to a matter which is not within our present scope – the quality of government lawyers. In fact, its manifestations are much broader, and bear directly on the Washington lawyer himself. To state the matter summarily, one of the very important reasons why we do have able government lawyers – why the scales are not weighted as the Justice feared they would be – is that we have permitted government lawyers to leave the government and become Washington lawyers in private practice. Now, at least, the limitations imposed on the ex-government lawyer, while not ideal, are reasonable. The danger, however, which warrants some attention to the problem, is that recent developments will lead us into indiscriminate measures, which will seriously prejudice both the government lawyer and the private practitioner.

The danger arises from an aspect of Washington life which has been much in the news of late. "Influence-peddling" is not a very accurate term, and it covers a multitude of sins, but it is sufficiently descriptive to define what we are talking about. It has been publicized and condemned, and in some respects misunderstood. What I should like to suggest is that in our efforts to control lawyers who engage in it we do not adopt such drastic restrictions on the ex-government lawyer as to make it difficult, or impossible, for the government to continue to attract able lawyers for service in its legal positions.

To make my point clear, we must have a little background. There are a few matters on which all should agree. First, no one doubts that it is important to have competent lawyers in government. Where safeguards of the adversary sort do not exist, it will fall to the government official – frequently, the government lawyer – to see to it that there is an adequate consideration of all the sides of the question. That cannot be expected if only the waifs and strays of the legal profession – the lawyers who can't get jobs elsewhere because of their inadequate training or their basic incompetence – are the ones who serve the public. We cannot decree the protection of the public interest by requiring those who want Washington counsel to retain only lawyers whose earnings are no more than the men they deal with in the government, nor can we have a Public Defender to make an adversary proceeding out of every petition for permission to adjust wage rates, or every negotiated government contract. We can best serve ourselves by securing the best servants we can afford.

Second, I believe that we can agree that we do get very many competent lawyers in government, even with the low government salary scale. One of the reasons is the security of the position; short of a catastrophe, one can reasonably expect long tenure in any but the highest government legal positions. Another reason, too, especially in times like these, is patriotism. Many lawyers, some of whom can ill afford it, are making financial sacrifices because they did not feel that they could say no to a request for their services. Another reason is that in many ways the work is interesting, even exciting, and for many government lawyers there is a strong belief in the rightness of the institutions with which they are associated and the purpose of the statutes with which they deal. *Esprit de corps* is not an exclusive with the military.

These factors operate, with varying force, on all government employees. For lawyers in particular, another factor seems to me of even more importance. There has been a recognition, at least since the early 1930's, that legal ability is of more value to the government than legal experience. Most departments have operated on the wise premise that an appropriation of $10,000 can be better spent to employ three able young lawyers with $10,000 worth of ability, even if they are just out of law school, rather than to employ one older, experienced man. Consequently, Washington has been a strong magnet for young lawyers of very high talents, who could get pay as high or higher than they could command on entering private practice, and who would promptly be assigned to positions of considerable responsibility.

This is in essence a process of earning while learning. Its necessary correlative is that these young lawyers must later be able to use in private practice what they have learned. This they have done; a goodly proportion of Washington lawyers have served, for longer or shorter periods, in some government legal position.

I trust that the reader concurs with me in rejecting the charge, which has recently been made, that this cheats the government because it is being used as a postgraduate legal course. Every lawyer handling a particular type of case for the first time learns as he does it, and can profit by that learning in similar cases later. There is no suggestion in this that he has cheated the first client, or that he should avoid charging a fee for his first venture into any new problem. The mature, experienced lawyer who commands large fees because of his experience got that way by charging fees for each, or most, of the cases which went to enrich his maturity. Moreover – and I think this is an equally valid answer – the government gets more than it gives; the quality of government legal talent has been remarkably high for the price which it pays.

Third, let us agree that influence-peddling in its various forms does exist. It is an area in which the difficulties of obtaining adequate information are obvious. All of us know, however, that Washington, particularly present-day Washington, is an irresistible lure to those who can hold themselves out as having connections, special entrees, inside tracks, and all the other trappings of the influence-peddler. This has nothing to do with whether the administration is Democratic or Republican, or with the particular men who compose that administration. The influence-peddler is attracted because the federal government in Washington is now the most gigantic and all-pervading government we have ever known. It is the country's largest banker. Through its vaults flow at least one quarter of the total national income. Indeed, the dollars which it collects and spends, and the way in which it collects and spends them, are the most significant facts in our economy. Moreover, for many very substantial industries the full power of economic life or death is wielded by Washington agencies such as the Civil Aeronautics Board, the Federal Power Commission, the Maritime Administration, the Tariff Commission, and in an emergency period, for any user of critical materials, the National Production Authority and its related bodies.

Favor seekers, and those who cater to them, are

an inevitable concomitant. With every indication, or even suspicion, that "influence" is occasionally effective, the pressure increases on the average person who has dealings with the government to seek a similar solution.

Much as one would like to say the contrary, Washington lawyers no doubt have their share of influence-peddlers. Some are simply unscrupulous, some have only a warped sense of ethics, and a particularly thick skin. Just how far the debasement of the professional standards of the legal profession has gone, I cannot even guess.

Of course, this does not mean that everyone who peddles influence has it. Quite the contrary. Probably 999 times out of 1000 a client who employs a Washington lawyer who claims to have influence doesn't get what he thinks he does, and what he pays for. At best he gets a guide through the Washington labyrinth that any Washington lawyer can give him, or perhaps a hearing on his problem with a government official who might be difficult to see without an appointment. At worst, he gets less than nothing; his case is tainted by the ill-will with which most government employees will regard a known or apparent influence-peddler.

Even if he escapes that, he probably gets nothing in the way of assistance, for the lawyer who is in the business of selling influence is either *ipso facto* incompetent or is not likely to trouble his mind about supplying helpful professional advice.

So much, then, for the background. Assuming agreement on those three points, let us consider what, if any, corrective measures are in order. There are many possibilities, and I do not propose to attempt a discussion of them all. The one which is relevant to our present topic is the current suggestion that we can minimize influence-peddling by more severe limitations on ex-government lawyers. If I am correct, and I am sure that I am, that a major attraction of government law practice to able young lawyers is an ability to utilize later what they learn in government, it is clear that we must move with caution or we may do irreparable harm. We have already gone quite a way in legislating ethical canons. Legislative control of morals, however, is dubious business at best, and in attempting to legislate against the occasional lawyer whose regard for the Canon of Ethics is minimal or nonexistent, we may well, as one article has stated, "surround the government service with so many snares, snags and spring-guns that only the unwary can be recruited."[10] It will be worth while to see whether the laws and regulations can be improved and strengthened, without at the same time putting the government lawyer who wants to enter private practice at such a disadvantage that few will be willing to serve in the first place.

At the present time, there are two major permanent statutes. The principal one[11] makes it a crime for a lawyer who has worked for the government to prosecute "any claim" against the government for two years after leaving government service if the claim involves "any subject matter directly connected with" the work in which the lawyer was employed or performed duty.

The statute has two weaknesses, both of which can be corrected without undue limitation on the Washington lawyer and without jeopardizing the attraction of government legal service. The word "claims," which defines what the lawyer may not prosecute, is open to the very narrow construction that it applies only to monetary claims. That is a wholly unnecessary and formalistic limitation. The real weakness of the statute, however, lies deeper. The real defect is that the law should appear to sanction a violation of Canon 36 of the Canons of Professional Ethics. That Canon provides:

> A lawyer, having once held public office or having been in the public employ, should not after his retirement accept employment in connection with any matter which he has investigated or passed upon while in such office or employ.

There is no limit as to time in Canon 36, and there should not be in the statute. Government does not move fast enough to warrant a legislative finding that things will always be different after two years.

The other statute applicable to ex-government lawyers, while more sweeping in its terms, has had but limited effect.[12] It forbids, for two years, a lawyer employed in any of the executive departments from prosecuting any claim against the government which was pending while he was employed. This is much too drastic, even if the word "claim" is construed narrowly, and it also contains the unfortunate two-year limitation. That it has not had more serious consequences is due to the fact that it carries no specific criminal sanctions, and has been applied only to prevent the lawyer from collecting a fee.[13]

There is room here for improvement. There

should be a permanent, rather than a temporary, ban on work by an ex-government lawyer so far as he may be involved in matters on which he worked while in the government. There are difficulties in the application of the phrase "matters on which he worked," and the language of the law should be carefully drawn to make the penumbra of doubtful cases as narrow as possible. Canon 36, which says about all there is need to say on the subject, is probably important enough in this area to be accorded criminal sanctions.

Indeed, it might be well to go further, and extend the permanent prohibition to representation before the agencies of government in any matters in connection with which the government lawyer had any immediate responsibility during his government employment. This is the approach that has been adopted in the Executive Order issued under Section 710 of the Defense Production Act of 1950.[14] Here there are no doubt palpable and considerable subsequent disadvantages which might affect the quality of the upper stratum of government legal services. Nevertheless, lawyers in top government positions do have supervisory relationships which may affect problems being worked on by their subordinates, even though they do not have any direct contact with the matters themselves. If the law is carefully drawn, a more substantial limitation on lawyers who had wider government responsibilities would help materially to eliminate unfortunate intangible effects.

To meet this same problem there is also room for a temporary prohibition. Canon 36 does not cover the abuse of friendships and residual prestige of the lawyer who held a high place in the government. Senator Douglas's subcommittee, in reporting on "Ethical Standards in Government," concludes that "A public official of high rank who leaves a regulatory agency and then returns immediately to practice before it, can hardly avoid pleading with people who previously may have been his subordinates or associates."[15] The Committee recommended a two-year "sterilization" period, during which persons who had held a position in an agency with a grade of GS–15 or above ($10,000 per year or more) would be barred from acting before the agency in any matter whatever.[16] One might doubt whether the line is not drawn at a point somewhat too far down on the scale, but there appears to be justification for a rule which distinguishes on the one hand the situation of the lawyer who held an important place in the government, and on the other the situation of the vast body of government lawyers whose area of work and responsibility is limited in scope, and whose future livelihood may well depend on the right to continue to make use of their experience.

Finally, there is need for administrative regulations and enforcement of ethical standards. Because so many Washington lawyers are not members of the local bar, the only Grievance Committee to which they are amenable is that of their own bar, which may be remote, uninformed, and even uninterested. There is need for something equivalent to a local Washington Grievance Committee for such lawyers. This could be met by the general adoption of a regulation such as that of the Securities and Exchange Commission, which provides that the privilege of practicing before it may be denied to anyone who after hearing is found to be "lacking in character or integrity or to have engaged in unethical or improper professional conduct." [17]

But let us recognize that no matter how we perfect and refine the rules, we cannot legislate a moral attitude or a cure for influence-peddling. All influence-peddlers are by no means ex-government employees, and no statute or regulation will ever take the place of an individual sense of concern for moral standards and ethical conduct. Moreover, we must recognize that there is a distinction between influence-peddling and what, for lack of a better word, we may call reputation, or expertise. Any Washington lawyer who is worth his salt and who has practiced in Washington for any length of time will have at least a speaking acquaintance with many of the staff in any agency where he may specialize. If he has professional competence and individual integrity – if he is a good lawyer in the true sense of the words – he will not only be known, he will be known favorably. That status will give him undoubted advantages – it will make it easier for him to arrange a conference, or to obtain a hearing for his client, or to discuss and discover the agency's position on particular matters that may come up. The lawyer who appeared in that agency for the first time would not find similar achievements impossible, and his client would fare equally well, if sufficient perseverance were exerted and if sufficient time were available. But advantages based on reputation and experience are wholly normal and wholly proper. To condemn them is likewise to condemn the trial lawyer in Chicago whose clients are advantaged because he is known to the court clerks and familiar with the intimate workings of their offices.

Thus far, we have been dealing with the relationship between the Washington lawyer and the government, and some of its attendant problems, when the lawyer is representing clients. There remains the second feature of his governmental activity, when he appears in *propria persona.* To say that lawyers generally have such a role to play – indeed, such a responsibility – is simply to acknowledge that they are not only citizens, but members of a profession having special qualifications for public affairs. And this is so both in relation to their community and in relation to their government.

When we focus on the activities of the Washington lawyer, however, as a citizen and as a professional man, we find an immediate dichotomy is needed. At least, that is true in the city of Washington. The Washington lawyers who practice in that city exhibit, in their relationship to each other and to the community, a pronounced lack of cohesiveness and of integration with their locality. On the other hand, in their relation to and impact on government itself, they are active and important. Both of these aspects will repay a more detailed examination.

In describing the relationship of the Washington lawyer, in Washington, to his brethren and to the District of Columbia, I should make it clear at the outset that I have no purpose to imply that Washington lawyers are consciously shirking or avoiding what Chief Justice Stone has called "the social objects of the profession." The cumulative effect of a number of factors has simply created, perhaps inevitably, a different sort of bar.

One factor, and an obvious one, is the relative newness of the group. To the extent that materials permit, that has already been discussed and requires no further comment. One need only say that the importance of this factor should not be overestimated, since there seems to have been no significant change in conditions during the past two decades.

Another and more significant factor is the nature of the community — of Washington — insofar as it is *not* the federal government. Washington has no large industrial concentration, and many of its citizens are temporary and transient residents — twenty years of Democratic administration to the contrary notwithstanding. Its residents and its local industries have their own problems with the federal government — their taxes, their price regulations, their labor disputes and the like — but local problems would not, and do not, support the Washington lawyers. Their clients are drawn from throughout the United States and its possessions; indeed, with the development of Washington as a world capital, they may well be drawn from throughout the world. The consequence is that Washington lawyers function almost in local anonymity. There are exceptions, but there are also many Washington lawyers who have entered the group by way of prominent public positions and who now have large and highly successful Washington practices, and yet remain almost unknown except to their local partners, their personal friends and their numerous but widely-scattered clients.

Also tending to separate the Washington lawyers from the community is the relatively high proportion among them of strangers to Washington. Very many Washington lawyers have seen service with the federal government in Washington in some capacity before entering private practice. They naturally reflect the nation-wide recruitment of personnel by the government itself. More than that, the seemingly greater interest and excitement of Washington practice has attracted law graduates from all over the United States. In the largest Washington firm, for example, only 3 of 70 lawyers were born in the District of Columbia, and only 13 of the 70 went to one of the several District of Columbia law schools. Whether this is typical is perhaps open to some question, but certainly there are in Washington many lawyers who have neither roots in the District, nor even the local acquaintanceship and clientele which attendance at the local law schools might give. Indeed, the District of Columbia law schools themselves tend strongly and consciously in the direction of being national law schools in the pattern of Harvard or Yale.

These aliens transplanted in Washington retain much of their alienage. They donate, of course, to the Community Chest, to the National Symphony Orchestra, and other local causes; they belong to clubs and to local churches; but their professional cohesiveness and relationship to the community is peculiarly absent. Their interest in the community is diluted because of their retained interests in their states of origin, where not infrequently they remain important. That Washington has no local self-government, and no right to vote for any candidate for public office, impels many of its residents to maintain their voting residences elsewhere, with the normal interests and attachments to the state in which they vote. This matter of a voting right is more than a casual one; it is a matter of pride and satisfaction that one may still vote, no matter how long he has lived in the District of Columbia, and no matter even that in some cases the price of a voting residence is a liability for extra local taxes.

There is another factor, too, which accentuates both the detachment of the lawyer from the community, and his detachment from his fellows. This is the fact which I have already mentioned – that a Washington lawyer need not be, and frequently is not, a member of the bar of the District Court for the District of Columbia. He may be a member of the bar of the Court of Appeals for the District, which is itself a quasi-national court and which does not require, as a condition to membership, a membership in the local District Court. True, such an attorney may not practice before the local courts, and occasionally he may encounter a federal agency or department which has conditioned admission to practice before it on membership by the applicant in the bar of the locality in which the attorney's office is located. On the whole, however, the Washington lawyer, provided he is admitted to some bar, somewhere, can carry on his day-to-day affairs without the slightest concern with the bar of which he seems to be a member.

The truth is that Washington lawyers are a singularly unorganized and unorganizable group. Even to call them a group is misleading, for they are actually no more than a number of individuals whose organization and interrelation stop almost completely at the limit of their own firms. They have none of the cohesiveness which comes from the common interests and frequent contacts of the local bar. For the Washington lawyer, the "lawyer on the other side" is almost always in the government; hence they lack the opportunity to develop that fraternity with each other which comes even from vigorous opposition to one another in court or in negotiation. Washington lawyers are disposed like the spokes of a wheel. They practice down the spokes against the hub which is the common opponent – the government – but seldom do their activities extend to what is doing on another spoke, even though it be only next door or across the street. What cohesiveness there is stems largely from the fact that as former government lawyers, many Washington lawyers were once at the hub of the wheel and became more or less widely acquainted in that capacity.

This discreteness, this lack of cohesion, is emphasized by what Chief Justice Stone called the "inevitable specialization of the Bar." Almost every Washington lawyer is a specialist. The Martindale-Hubbell Law Directory abounds, it is true, in statements of qualifications such as "Practice before all Courts and all Government Departments and Agencies." These representations are made not only by large firms which can agglomerate enough particular specialists to qualify; they are made, not infrequently, by small firms and even by individual lawyers. We have already seen enough of the differences in administrative practice, however, to appreciate that any Washington lawyer would admit that he can do a better job for his client before an agency, or in an area, where he has had prior experience.

All of these factors have far too much force to be overcome by the only sort of an organization which might integrate Washington lawyers with the community and with each other — the Bar Association.

The District of Columbia Bar Association has had a long and distinguished history, but from its founding in 1871 to the present time I suspect that few who could be called Washington lawyers, as we have used that term, have served as its presidents. Naturally and properly, the District of Columbia Bar Association has concerned itself principally with matters which affect the people of Washington, its government, its courts, its police, and the like. The Washington lawyer has taken, at best, a passive interest. There have been enthusiastic and repeated efforts on both sides — to expand the interests of the Association to encompass the wider interests of the Washington lawyer, and to expand the interests of the Washington lawyers in local bar association affairs — but these efforts have not as yet accomplished as much as one would like.

When we turn to the Washington lawyer's activities — sans client — in relation to the processes of federal government, we find a wholly different picture. In suggesting earlier that further study of agency procedures would be fruitful, I mentioned that some work of that nature had already been done. For example, a representative committee of industry counsel has functioned as a Civil Aeronautics Board Advisory Committee on Practices and Procedures. On an equally broad basis, the Committee on the Federal Trade Commission Act of the Section on Antitrust Law of the New York State Bar Association has developed, through informal meetings with the members and staff of the Federal Trade Commission, a number of suggestions for improvement, such as more clearly articulated rules of procedure, more specific definition of the powers of trial examiners, an increase in the number of written opinions by the Commission, and the like. And again, in the District of Columbia Bar Association, a Committee on Emergency Agencies of the Administrative Law Section has made a critical survey of the procedures of the present defense agencies, and has secured the adoption of several improvements.

Nor do I mean to overlook the more massive achievements, such as the Administrative Procedure Act, which was in large measure drafted by and enacted through the efforts of Washington lawyers in all parts of the United States. In much the same category is the complete and drastic revision of the rules of the Court of Claims, on which a distinguished group of practitioners before that court were advisers. Indeed, the examples are legion. Taken as a group, the Washington lawyers, in Washington and throughout the United States, have given generously of their time and ability to assist the government in bettering its standards, its procedures and its rules.

Before I leave the topic, however, I should like to devote a few remarks to an aspect of modern federal government in which the contributions of the bar have fallen far short of what I believe the public has a right to expect. This area concerns the federal loyalty program.

The loyalty program is a subject on which feelings run high. It would not be within the bounds of the topic under discussion to enter into the dispute over the extent to which the progam is a confession of a lack of faith in our fundamental ideas of freedom. It is appropriate, however, to take note of the failure of the bar to acknowledge its responsibility for ensuring that so long as there is a program, it be consistent with the traditions of due process which have been at once our security, our pride and our heritage. The program fairly bristles with problems.

Yet to my knowledge, not until March, 1952, did the bar begin any concerted effort to apply to those problems its collective wisdom and judgment in an effort at improvement.

The problems, of course, are not easy, nor do I claim to know the answers to them. That the problems are insoluble, however, is a confession of defeat which we dare not make, and that they are already solved is a confession of complacency which is belied not only by the fact of a Supreme Court equally divided on certain of the issues of procedural due process in the *Bailey* case,[18] but also by the sobering arguments of eminent Americans who cannot be ignored.[19]

Take, for example, the definition of what it is the Loyalty Boards are to determine. All of us will agree that no one who is disloyal should serve his country. The President's loyalty order makes the standard for dismissal of an employee the existence of a reasonable doubt that he is "loyal to the government of the United States." Yet no one can doubt that "loyalty" is an intensely personal matter, manifested in widely different ways, and incapable of simple or even universal measurement. What is evidence of disloyalty to one member of a Loyalty Board may be irrelevant, or even evidence of loyalty, to another member. What a government employee may do or should not do consistent with his loyalty pledge is impossible of prior determination. The Socialists, for example, though bitterly opposed to, and by, the Communists, are by many equated with the Communists as equally disloyal. Probably a wise government employee should not actively support the Socialist ticket. Can we not devise a definition of those whom we wish to eliminate from our government service which will better serve to protect both our government and our tradition of heterodoxy?

Even more disturbing are the procedural deficiencies. Justices Holmes and Brandeis have pointed out that "in the development of our liberty insistence upon procedural regularity has been a large factor."[20] As Francis Biddle has said:

> . . . Procedure has been to a very great extent the threshold of our freedoms, the palpable issue around which the specific struggles have been waged. Jury trial, habeas corpus, the right to appeal, the right of confrontation of witnesses, protection from double jeopardy and against unlawful searches and seizures —

these are procedural safeguards, and without them our substantive rights become shadowy and sterile.[21]

We have an obligation, as members of the legal profession, to examine these procedural problems. That one may decide on the unwisdom of complete disclosure of every counter-espionage agent in every loyalty case does not mean that we need go to the other extreme and maintain an almost total anonymity of accusers or adverse witnesses. That specification of charges may necessarily be limited in occasional instances by security considerations does not mean that sweeping, general allegations should be the rule. That it might be unwise to permit an unlimited right in the accused to subpoena witnesses does not mean that the right to subpoena should be wholly denied. Is there not a need for a fundamental reexamination of the concept of guilt by association? These are basic matters, where a whittling away of safeguards is portentous for us all.

Let me illustrate where we now stand by an example. The Administrative Procedure Act did more than enact strictly procedural safeguards, it also enacted safeguards against any loss of integrity of the hearing examiners — the administrative judges. To insure against improper pressures upon them in matters in which examiners were called upon to decide between the agency and the persons who were in contest with it, Section 11 of that Act provides that no examiner can be removed by the agency, but only by the Civil Service Commission, and then only after a fair hearing. Section 11 spells out enough of the basic minima of the hearing procedures to insure that it be fair, and that the decision be based strictly upon the merits of the case.

Recently the Civil Service Commission advised Congress that loyalty reports had been received as to certain hearing examiners, which in the ordinary case would require a loyalty hearing. Adverting to the minimum procedural requirements of Section 11 for a fair hearing, the Commission stated:

> [In this situation the Commission is left] in a dilemma. If the Administrative Procedure Act is not followed . . . any adjudication of disloyalty is sure to be reversed in a subsequent proceeding in court.
>
> If the Administrative Procedure Act is followed, the evidence that can be presented at the hearing is certain to be insufficient to justify adjudication of disloyalty.[22]

Is there not cause for concern in that statement — in the frank acknowledgment that the loyalty program cannot operate under fair hearing procedures?

Should we not examine carefully into a situation where a statute which has justly been regarded as a milestone in the development of decent administrative procedure is an obstacle to a loyalty conviction? Should not the bar, and particularly the Washington bar, whose experience in loyalty cases probably exceeds that of all others, concern itself with this ominous dilemma?

We should not have made it necessary for the President to appeal to the lawyers for assistance; we should have been alert to our own traditions and responsibilities. Mr. Truman, after describing the loyalty and security program, said in his letter of September, 1951, to the American Bar Association:

> All these measures and proposed measures should be given critical, constructive, and public consideration by the bar to help our people and the authorities involved determine whether they are reasonable and practical methods of maintaining security or whether their potentialities in terms of stifling freedom of expression outweigh their utility as security measures. Searching scrutiny of this character by able and fair-minded lawyers will greatly contribute toward enlightening the whole Nation as to how we can best strike the difficult balance between security and individual rights in these trying times. Your contributions will be all the greater

if you give the matter continuous and detailed attention and make your conclusions widely known.[23]

Belatedly, the following March, the American Bar Association approved the creation of a "Special Committee on Individual Rights as Affected by National Security." The federal loyalty program had then been in operation for almost five years, but until the President's plea was made, the principal reaction of the American Bar Association to the loyalty program was a resolution requesting the appropriate authorities in each state to impose a periodic test oath,[24] and a later resolution calling for the prompt institution of disbarment proceedings against "all lawyers who are members of the Communist Party of the United States, or who advocate Marxism or Leninism."[25] Its special committee, in recommending the latter resolution, as well as a test oath for all members of the Association, stated its feeling "that by the adoption of this resolution the bar will be able to face the American people with pride."[26] I venture to suggest that we could have taken far more pride in a record which would have evidenced not a desire to show that lawyers can purge with the best of them, but rather that we have left no stone unturned to insure that the loyalty program is as fully consistent with our ancient liberties as its unique problems will permit.

In conclusion, may I venture one more thought. I have written of the Washington lawyer somewhat as if he were a laboratory specimen, but there is a good deal more to him than that. Not only does he engage in the type of practice which I have tried to outline; not only does he have his particular problems and his particular characteristics; not only does he contribute substantially to better and more equitable government; but also, and probably of just as much importance, he finds it pleasurable as well as profitable. I know of few Washington lawyers who do not regard their day-to-day practice as interesting or even exciting, challenging and rewarding. The particular problem on which one may be working is perhaps a matter of detail — indeed, of infinitely small detail — but it usually requires an understanding of a larger problem of which it is a part, and since the larger problems are those on which we stake a considerable part of our economic and political future, it is impossible to avoid, even if you would, an intimate sense of participation in significant affairs.

By saying this I do not intend to belittle any other type of law practice. Every lawyer, no matter what his practice may be, must obtain a full measure of satisfaction from his work. The Washington lawyer seldom derives the warm satisfaction that comes from the more intimate association with men and women whose problems are personal and whose fortunes, well-being and even lives may depend upon the lawyer's ability to obtain for them equal and even-handed justice. For the Washington lawyer, whose contacts are more likely to be with problems rather than people, the compensations of his practice are simply of a somewhat different order. Perhaps this adds up to confessing that I enjoy it.

Notes

I. GENERAL CHARACTERISTICS OF WASHINGTON PRACTICE; JUDICIAL AND LEGISLATIVE ACTIVITIES

[1] The figures given are based on statistics compiled from the Martindale-Hubbell Law Directory (1949 ed.) and Nofer and Hildebrand, Statistical Report on the Lawyers of the United States (1949). A second report is being prepared for publication in 1952. See also Blaustein, "The 1949 Lawyear Count: A Preliminary Statement," 36 A.B.A.J. 370 (1950).

[2] Swaine, The Cravath Firm 713 (1948).

[3] Sereni, "Italy's Legal Profession," 63 Harv. L. Rev. 1000, 1004 (1950).

[4] The State of Society in France before the Revolution of 1789, 153 (3d ed., Reeve trans., 1888).

[5] By its third term, in 1865, although 19 attorneys appear in its 41 reported decisions, 2 of them appear in 25 of the cases. The following year, 26 attorneys appear in the same number of reported decisions, but 4 attorneys and one other firm again appear in over half of the cases. By 1867, the decisions have expanded to over 80, but the bulk of the practice is confined to fewer than a dozen lawyers.

[6] An analysis of the cases handled by a large Washington law firm in the decade from 1920 to 1930 shows the dominance of tax practice, and the relative proportion of nongovernment work. There is no assurance, of course, that it is typical.

1920–1923 (401 cases)

Tax cases	112
Other government cases	112
(E.g., claims against the government, 18; Alien Property Custodian matters, 14; immigration and naturalization, 30; tariff, 3; copyright, 6; antitrust, 5; legislation, 6; international matters, 5)	
Nongovernment cases	106
Not classified	66

1923–1926 (763 cases)

Tax cases	320
Other government cases	64
Nongovernment cases	122
Not classified	257

1926–1930 (795 cases)

Tax cases	405
Other government cases	120
Nongovernment cases	228
Not classified	42

[7] "In 8 Cranch (1812–1813), of the forty-six cases in which names of counsel are given, Pinkney argued in exactly one half." 1 Warren, The Supreme Court in United States History 566 n.3 (1926).

[8] Warren, A History of the American Bar 368 (1911). Mr. Warren also notes the large number of Supreme Court cases argued at that time by members of Congress. Id. at 413; The Supreme Court in United States History, vol. I, p. 23 (1926).

[9] 1 Warren, The Supreme Court in United States History 674 (1926).

[10] In 1950, there were 45 petitions filed in the Court of Appeals for the District of Columbia from boards and commissions other than the National Labor Relations Board, while only 25 were filed in all other circuits. For the five-year period 1946–1950, 151 were filed in the District of Columbia, 130 elsewhere. Annual Report of the Director of the Administrative Office of the United States Courts, 1950, pp. 132–34.

[11] In re Chapman, 166 U.S. 661 (1897).

[12] 103 U.S. 168 (1880). In the Sugar Trust Cases the Supreme Court upheld the power of Congress to inquire into charges that members of the Senate were yielding to corrupt influences in consideration of a tariff bill; in the Kilbourn case the Court denied that Congress could constitutionally inquire into the history and character of a "real estate pool" in the District of Columbia, then involved in bankruptcy litigation in the courts.

[13] General Interim Report, House Select Committee on Lobbying Activities, H.R. Rep. No. 3138, 81st Cong., 2d Sess. 1 (1950).

[14] Act of July 25, 1946, 60 Stat. 664.

[15] Act of May 14, 1947, 61 Stat. 84.

[16] 328 U.S. 680 (1946).

[17] Overnight Motor Transportation Co. v. Missel, 316 U.S. 572 (1942); Brooklyn Savings Bank v. O'Neil, 324 U.S. 697 (1945).

[18] See Jones, "Bill-Drafting Services in Congress and the State Legislatures," 65 Harv. L. Rev. 441 (1952).

[19] Hearings before a Subcommittee of the House Committee on the Merchant Marine and Fisheries on Alaskan Fisheries pursuant to H. Res. 28, 79th Cong., 2d Sess., part 1

(1946). See also Report of Dept. of Interior on H.R. 3859, June 11, 1947, House Merchant Marine and Fisheries Comm. Doc. No. 87.

II. ACTIVITIES RELATING TO THE EXECUTIVE BRANCH AND THE ADMINISTRATIVE AGENCIES

[1] Austern, "The Formulation of Mandatory Food Standards," 2 Food Drug Cosmetic L.Q. 532, 533 (1947).

[2] Final Report (1941) Sen. Doc. No. 8, 77th Cong., 1st Sess. 7–11.

[3] "Administrative Law: A Practical Attitude for Lawyers," 25 A.B.A.J. 275, 277 (1939).

[4] "Public Service by the Bar," 41 A.B.A. Rep. 355, 368–69 (1916).

[5] Dulles, "Administrative Law: A Practical Attitude for Lawyers," 25 A.B.A.J. 275–76 (1939). See also Final Report, Attorney General's Committee on Administrative Procedure, Sen. Doc. No. 8, 77th Cong., 1st Sess. 13–14 (1941).

[6] Griffith, "Law and Continuous Investigation," 31 Am. Lab. Leg. Rev. 149 (1941).

[7] 1 Jessup, Elihu Root 132–133 (1938).

[8] Fishgold v. Sullivan Drydock & Repair Corp., 154 F.2d 785 (2d Cir. 1946), affirmed, 328 U.S. 275 (1946). See also Bay Ridge Operating Co. v. Aaron, 334 U.S. 446, 453–454 (1948), and Powell v. United States Cartridge Co., 339 U.S. 497, 530 (1950), which reflect the same conflict between separate federal agencies.

[9] See Loss, Securities Regulation 334–340 (1951).

[10] Darrell, "Recent Developments in Nontaxable Reorganizations and Stock Dividends," 61 Harv. L. Rev. 958 (1948); DeWind, "Preferred Stock 'Bail-Outs' and the Income Tax," 62 Harv. L. Rev. 1126 (1949).

[11] See Universal Camera Corp. v. National Labor Relations Board, 340 U.S. 474 (1951).

[12] 50 U.S.C.A. App. § 1218 (1946).

[13] Morgan v. United States, 298 U.S. 468 (1936), 304 U.S. 1 (1938), 307 U.S. 183 (1939), 313 U.S. 409 (1941).

[14] Hand, "Thomas Walter Swan," 57 Yale L.J. 167, 169 (1947).

[15] Davis, Administrative Law 137–138 (1951).

[16] Newman, "Government and Ignorance – A Progress Report on Publication of Federal Regulations," 63 Harv. L. Rev. 929 (1950).

[17] 16 Fed. Reg. 2932 (1951).

[18] Ewing v. Mytinger & Casselberry, Inc., 339 U.S. 594 (1950).

III. SOME REFLECTIONS ON THE ROLE OF THE WASHINGTON LAWYER

[1] 48 Harv. L. Rev. 1 (1934).

[2] Id. at 6–7.

[3] Schwegmann Bros. v. Calvert Distillers Corp., 341 U.S. 384, 395–397 (1951), concurring.

[4] Miller, "The Successful Tax Lawyer – His Character and Personal Relationships," 7 Tax. L. Rev. 9 (1951).

[5] Swaine, "Impact of Big Business on the Profession: An Answer to Critics of the Modern Bar," 35 A.B.A.J. 89, 170–171 (1949).

[6] "The Opportunity in the Law," 39 Am. L. Rev. 555 (1905).

[7] Id. at 561.

[8] Fishgold v. Sullivan Drydock & Repair Corp., 154 F.2d 785, 789 (2d Cir. 1946), affirmed, 328 U.S. 275 (1946).

See also Stern, "'Inconsistency' in Government Litigation," 64 Harv. L. Rev. 759 (1951).

[9] Schwegmann Bros. v. Calvert Distillers Corp., 341 U.S. 384 (1951), holding that under the Miller-Tydings Act a manufacturer could not enforce prescribed minimum resale prices against a retailer who had not agreed to maintain such prices, even though the state law purported to bind him along with those retailers who had signed agreements to maintain minimum prices.

[10] McElwain and Vorenberg, "The Federal Conflict of Interest Statutes," 65 Harv. L. Rev. 955 (1951).

[11] 18 U.S.C. § 284 (Supp. 1951): "*Disqualification of former officers and employees in matters connected with former duties.* Whoever, having been employed in any agency of the United States, including commissioned officers assigned to duty in such agency, within two years after the time when such employment or service has ceased, prosecutes or acts as counsel, attorney, or agent for prosecuting, any claims against the United States involving any subject matter directly connected with which such person was so employed or performed duty, shall be fined not more than $10,000 or imprisoned not more than one year, or both."

[12] Rev. Stat. § 190 (1875), 5 U.S.C. § 99 (1946): "*Ex-officers or employees not to prosecute claims in departments.* It shall not be lawful for any person appointed as an officer, clerk, or employee in any of the departments, to act as counsel, attorney, or agent for prosecuting any claim against the United States which was pending in either of said departments while he was such officer, clerk, or employee, nor in any manner, nor by any means, to aid in the prosecution of any such claim, within two years next after he shall have ceased to be such officer, clerk, or employee."

[13] E.g., Van Metre v. Nunn, 116 Minn. 444, 133 N.W. 1012

(1912); Ludwig v. Raydure, 25 Ohio App. 293, 157 N.E. 816 (1927), cert. denied, 275 U.S. 545 (1927).

[14] Exec. Order No. 10,182, pt. II, 15 Fed. Reg. 8013 (1950), as amended.

[15] Report of a Subcommittee of the Senate Committee on Labor and Public Welfare, 82d Cong., 1st Sess. 22 (1951).

[16] Id. at 51–52.

[17] 17 Code Fed. Regs. §201.2(e)(2) (1949). This regulation was applied to a firm which was told it would violate Canon 36 if it permitted an ex-employee to work on a matter, wholly intra-office, on which he had worked while with the Commission. 3 CCH Fed. Sec. Law. Serv. ¶68,102.10 (1939).

[18] Bailey v. Richardson, 182 F.2d 46 (D.C. Cir. 1950) (two-to-one decision), affirmed by an equally divided Court, 341 U.S. 918 (1951).

[19] E.g., Biddle, The Fear of Freedom (1951); Barth, The Loyalty of Free Men (1951).

[20] Burdeau v. McDowell, 256 U.S. 465, 477 (1921) (dissenting).

[21] Biddle, op. cit. supra note 19, at 209.

[22] New York Times, Dec. 21, 1951, p. 14.

[23] Letter to the American Bar Association, reprinted in 97 Cong. Rec. 11983–84 (Sept. 20, 1951).

[24] 75 A.B.A. Rep. 148 (1950), reaffirmed, 37 A.B.A.J. 320 (1951).

[25] 37 A.B.A.J. 313 (1951).

[26] A.B.A. Brief on Communism: Marxism-Leninism, with Reports and Recommendations of the Special Committee on Communist Tactics, Strategy and Objectives, 1951, pp. 33–34, 52–53 (1951).

www.ingramcontent.com/pod-product-compliance
Ingram Content Group UK Ltd.
Pitfield, Milton Keynes, MK11 3LW, UK
UKHW041624031026
15587UKWH00001B/39

9 780313 227363